FEAR CRACKED OPEN

Unlocking the You that You deserve

EILEEN BUCHHEIT AND
BRENDA DEAN SHULL, PH.D.

-For our children and grandchildren who have given a lifetime of memories and laughter.

-For our friends (also sister Debra and brother Joe) who have remembered our song when we forgot the words.

-For our sweet husbands, David and Joe, who helped our resilience through life's challenges and kept a smile in our heart.

Dear Readers:

As Eileen and I were sitting on the porch of her Connecticut farm, laughing over some revisited memories, we knew we needed to write some of the humorous tales that laced our long friendship. Meeting fifty years ago, she was a brunette from Queens, New York, and I, a blond (roots don't count) from Dallas, Texas. She is Catholic and I am Protestant. Both of us were newly married and brides of newly commissioned men going into the Army when Viet Nam was still operative. We both spoke English, but it did not sound that way.

Our lives were not our mother's lives.

And so, we recounted much of this laughter and growth in our first book, "Christmas Countdown, Slightly Cracked."

However, Eileen and I knew there was another book to be written, peppered with personal humorous events. This book, borne out of our counseling, teaching and corporate experience as professionals, would be for women.

We knew that we and almost all women want to grow to our fullest potential, finding our purpose.

But we noticed that in different stages of life, this purpose had to be ***refined* or *redefined at each life stage.*** *Often our life stage changes our lives in surprising or unwanted directions.*

At that point, we must **redesign or decline!**

- One stage of life brings our education or career to the forefront.
- Another might be the decision to marry or have children.
- Another stage would be empty nesting or the loss of a partner.

At each stage, we must question, search deeper and redesign ourselves to live authentic lives. As Camus has said, "Life is a sum of all our choices."

Over and over, the decision would boil down to—did we want to be bitter or better?

Just as we thought we had the hang of partnering, working, or mothering, a new stage would develop.

Did we want to be angry at the change in life, or growth-enhanced?

Our purpose would be changed, whether we liked it or not, ready or not. Once again, the answer becomes clearer: "Redesign. Or Decline."

Eileen and I began to question what it was that holds women back from finding meaningful purpose in each of our life stages and relationships.

We recognized that it was irrational fear, not physical fear. Consequently, this book is not a discussion of physical fear. Nor are we describing ingrained complex mental health fears that need prolonged professional care.

Instead, we are discussing **irrational fears** that hold us back due to our hyperactive imagination.

These common fears limit us and keep us from becoming our authentic selves. In this book, we identify and shed light on these fears.

Allowing fear to drive our life and our decisions is like driving a car that only goes in reverse!

In this book we name fears, discuss fears and this book gives power over fears.

By distinguishing healthy from unhealthy, we are getting rid of distorted perceptions that contribute to pain. Growth and getting to the you that you deserve requires healing from tragedies or self-imposed limits that would keep us from wholeness.

Wholeheartedly we can say: Fear isolates. Trust transforms.

In this book, we expect fear to be replaced by recognition that what we are experiencing also happens to others as well. We give strategies to surge toward a unique purpose based on each stage of life experience.

Once we have helped you recognize what is holding you back by naming common fears, we offer a four-step model to create one's best self. It is based on the life of Jesus. Actionable behavioral exercises are offered to happily track you toward discovering that Purpose you desire.

Our bodies may age, but our authentic self can expand. (And we admit waistlines, too). Yes, this is self-help through discussion and a sense of humor.

When you shine light into the darkness, it is fear that flees.

Let's capture clarity over confusion, prayer over panic and faith over fear.

Come along. Let's step out of the blur into a clear vision of our best self no matter what life throws at you!

As Henry Ford said, "Whether you think you can, or think you can't, either way, you are right!"

Or as Martha Stewart who served as a Sports Illustrated cover model at the age of 81 has said, "If you are through with change, you are through with life."

Come journey with us. We will crack fear open.

Chapter One: **Fear, Cracked Open**

It was Friday night in Texas.

The quarterback was grandson of Jerry Jones, owner of the Dallas Cowboys. The team was going for the State championship in high school football.

Unfortunately, the team was losing. Four minutes were left on the clock.

My son with his young family were there supporting their neighborhood team. Looking at the clock, my son turned to his wife.

He did what many other loyal supporters do . . . Stand to his feet? Give louder cheers? Pump the air with his fist?

"Let's leave," he suggested, "so we can beat the traffic."

"What?" the others in the family moaned. With lingering sorrowful backward glances, all five of them made their way to the car. Vance flicked on the radio as they backed out from the packed parking lot.

"Wow," said the announcer on the radio. "You'd have to be stupid to be in the parking lot and miss that touchdown. We're now down by only three points. These guys are going for an offside kick to win the game."

And the team did the impossible.

They made that offside kick, made the touchdown, and won the State championship. Vance, unfortunately, like many others in the parking lot, couldn't believe that he missed it.

Isn't that life? So often, we are inches away from victory, but we quit due to a fear of our own making.

Often the darkest day is just before the gorgeous sunrise. It happened to the disciples and Mary Magdalene. Jesus had repeatedly told his followers that he would return on the third day. The disciples were scattered and fearful.

They had quit. Mary Magdalene was so defeated and upset as she came to the tomb that she did not recognize Jesus. She must have laughed the rest of her life as she recalled mistaking Jesus for the gardener. She was inches from the glorious sunrise of his resurrection and almost gave up too soon.

Inches from victory, we stop just short of our goal. What is it that holds us back? Too often it is fear.

There are physical fears. Adrenalin helps us get through a crisis, but long-term fear gets very tiring. For example, the coronavirus brought stress, anxiety, and fear on a global proportion. Pressing a pause button on our daily life, we hunkered down worldwide. During uncertainty, a new normal prevailed. We needed physical distance. For Easter or Christmas, we had to decide where to go—the living room or the kitchen to watch church online. Gas was finally affordable!

We were getting four WEEKS to the gallon. The streets were deserted. We learned not to worry about suspicious people on the sidewalk-- it was just our neighbors with no make-up and neglected haircuts in strange masks.

This fear was physical. Churches and schools closed, sports events cancelled, jobs shut down, but worst of all, hospitals were overwhelmed with dying patients throughout the globe.

Earlier, a physical fear had plagued women in the workplace which the #MeToo movement challenged. Feeling helpless in employment, women often thought that silence during physical harassment was a condition to be endured. Judgment, victim shaming, loss of job, and fear of retaliation made women stop short of many of their goals. Sometimes they were inches from victory.

Then, during the pandemic, another physical fear emerged. The devastating video emerged of a police officer in Minneapolis kneeling on the neck of George Floyd for nine minutes. America finally took notice of a very real fear that had plagued the Black community. Black mothers had previously warned their sons that a traffic stop could have fatal consequences.

Contemplating the hard truths of how racism and gender expectations have built fear, Eileen and Brenda began to seek some answers. What is the difference between physical fear and mental, irrational fears? It gets down to the basics--how does a female keep irrational fear from holding her back?
.
What keeps you awake at night? Most often, it is not physical fear that is keeping you awake, but mental fear! When we allow fear to have the upper hand, we do not need a "do not disturb" sign before dropping off to sleep. We are already mentally disturbed.

What are our greatest mental fears?

Jerry Seinfield said, "According to most studies, people's number one fear is **public speaking**. Number two is death. Death is number two. Does that sound right? This means to the average person, if you go to a funeral, you're better off in the casket than doing the eulogy."

That is not the number one fear for Brenda or Eileen. Think about what your number one fear is.

Brenda hates snakes. So, if you are walking through a grassy, rocky area, are you going to yell, "Watch out! It's a podium." When fear controls us, it is because we have imagined the worst!

Brenda had an up close and personal snake experience and yes, her imagination overshadowed any physical fear.

It was 11 PM on a Saturday night. She tells: My son and his wife had taken my granddaughter to Six Flags Amusement Park. They had not returned yet. I decided to lock the back door and prepare for bed. As I glanced out the door, I saw their kitty on the porch. "Here, Kitty, Kitty," I called. She ignored me.

Irritated, I stepped outside to grab her. That is when something snapped to my right.

Snap. Then plop. I looked down at my feet and less than six inches to my right foot was a coiled thick and wide snake. It looked like a python in a curled, coiled position. (This was one big snake!) The kitty had scared the snake up onto a ledge and the snake struck at me. The striking motion caused it to fall off the ledge, and land by my feet too close for comfort.

At that moment, I did what any rational person would do. I screamed and ran forward. It screamed and ran the opposite

4

direction. This means I dashed further onto my porch. This means it surged forward--into my house through the open door.

It was a dilemma. I was outside. It was inside, scooting toward . . . my bed. I knew that snake was thinking about hiding under my bed. All five feet of him. Or maybe it was six to seven feet? It gets longer in the re-telling. Coincidentally, my son's family returned. Together we analyzed the problem. With a round head, it must be a rat snake, non-poisonous. Yet, it was very, very large and happy under my bed. My son grabbed a shovel. The snake would not budge but would strike at the shovel.

Naturally we thought of the first responders! When the police officer arrived, I opened the door to see him holding a pitchfork-like device. His first words were, "I hate snakes." My answer was, "I do, too. Especially under my bed."

He replied, "Do you want him dead or alive." My answer was, "Alive since they are harmless. With that, this brave policeman reached under the bed, grasped him with the hook and raced past me with the snake flying like a 6-foot banner. Or was that seven feet? This meant I had to sleep in a bed that had previously had a snake under it. I had to take a flying leap to jump into the bed, so my toes did not touch underneath.

Rationally, Brenda knew the snake was not coming back. But, how do you have a peaceful night's sleep in that bed? Fear controls us if we imagine the worst. Brenda imagined the snake leaving snake babies, growing, coiling and emerging from under the bed. It was an irrational fear.

We have all done it. Irrational fear shows up when we imagine what MIGHT happen. Even in the best of times, we fear losing our job; but then, after a while, we fear getting stuck and keeping that job!

5

We fear losing our children; and then, we fear getting stuck and keeping those children long into their adult years.

We become afraid when change is in the air. Then we become afraid that there will be no change and we are stuck.
Here is an acronym for that kind of fear:
False
Events
Appearing
Real
I love another acronym that Adam Hamilton proposes in his book, "Unafraid."
Face your fears with faith.
Examine your assumptions in light of the facts.
Attack your anxieties with action
Release your cares to God.

Susan Stachler talks about this in "The Cookie Cure, A Mother-Daughter Memoir of Cancer to Cookies." She and her mom turned cancer into a cookie business. Susan was diagnosed with cancer when she graduated from college. Her mom heard that ginger is a natural stomach soother to help during chemotherapy. While her mom perfected the recipe, Susan worked on packaging. Susan says, "You don't know what's going to happen until it happens and that's a good thing. I had an idea of what I'd do after college and beating cancer and daily baking16,000 gingersnap cookies in the garage was certainly not my plan. . . isn't life full of surprises?"

Therefore, we have researched childhood, motherhood, marriage, singlehood and professional stages to find irrational fears that are holding us back. Maybe you'll recognize a few.

Chapter Two: Childhood Fears

"Don't worry about anything; instead, pray about everything.
Tell God what you need and thank him for all he has done.
Then you will experience God's peace, which exceeds anything
we can understand. His peace will guard your hearts and
minds as you live in Christ Jesus. " Philippians 4:6-7

Remember when you carefully dressed your precious little one
and took him to the long line in the Mall to have his picture
taken with Santa Claus?

You chatted casually. You pointed out the other children in
line while waiting your turn. You even mentioned the
peppermint candy that would probably be coming. Then, with
great pride you swung your child onto Santa's lap.

Your child takes one close look at that beard and the strange
red suit. Instantly, that sweet little face scrunches up into one
loud scream. Brenda says she now has a souvenir photo of her
son Justin's tonsils. He had a very loud and prolonged yelp
caught in the photo and was having nothing to do with this
very strange stranger. Eileen and Joe experienced the same

while taking their granddaughters Millie and JoJo to Disneyland. While Eileen was congratulating her hubby on how this expensive trip was worthwhile, a mouse creature approached their table at lunch. JoJo screamed in fear and could only be consoled by leaving lunch. It wasn't what she expected, nor did Brenda expect for her cherished child and Santa picture. Brenda had not realized that jolly old Santa could evoke such fear.

Children usually outgrow their fear of Santa. Pretty soon they are leaving cookies for the jolly old elf and his reindeer (cookies that Mom or Dad must choke down quickly on Christmas Eve.) Children learn to make their list or be good for the benefit of Santa's assistant Elf on the Shelf. However, there are some childhood fears that are not outgrown quickly and persist into adulthood. Let's review the most common researched fears of children and see if you can identify with some of them.

Fear of the dark is one of the most common fears of children. The National Association of Sleep Comfort and Coziness (NASCC) said 87% of adults admit that they won't sleep with their feet outside a blanket.

You never know when a night monster will pinch a toe. 11% of adult Americans are unable to get restful sleep in a totally darkened room. They still prefer night light. Eileen remembers her father arriving home late after his long day at work. He wanted to spend time with her and would lie on the bottom of the bed to talk with her. He would assure her that he would stay for a few minutes until she was fast asleep. Guess who fell asleep first. She remembers her feet were often trapped under the blanket. She thought if she moved, she would wake her well-meaning dad. As a result, she stayed awake and stiff until he woke up and left. Then, she could release her feet and fall asleep. To this day, she cannot sleep with her feet under a blanket even on the cold Connecticut nights. Nor did she ever tell her well- meaning dad that his action of love in keeping her from a fearful dark room was crushing her like a mummy.

Brenda was guilty of the same assumption. She assumed that this fear of the night was what plagued her then kindergarten granddaughter, Evelyn. Brenda said: One night when I was baby-sitting, we sat on her bed in her semi-dark room. We were surrounded by a puddle of night-time books that I had just finished reading to her. After the tenth book, I said, "Evelyn, you <u>must</u> be sleepy. It is time to go to sleep. What is it? Are you afraid of the dark?" She shook her head. "No, Gram. It's just that when I go to sleep, it means that soon I will wake up. That means I must go to school. I would really like to just stay home and play with my LOL dolls." Brenda in her adult mind had Evelyn's fears all wrong. Brenda had never thought of the explanation of being fearful of falling asleep because the ensuing wake- up meant going off to school.

It suddenly brought back memories that when Evelyn's dad was a kindergartener, he had hidden in the back seat of the carpool. It was quite a surprise for the driver to return home only to find a kindergartener in the back seat. Vance explained to the surprised driver that he would "much prefer staying at home with mommy." It took until first grade for both Vance and later his daughter to want to go to school.

.

This is a perfect example of how to help a child overcome fear.

First, by listening to the child, we may discover it is not the fear of the dark that we thought, but a fear of the unfamiliar, an active imagination or a stressful experience. A child is young and still discovering the world around them. Speaking to them and asking what makes them fearful may be the first step to understanding their world and their fear. Marie Curie, the first woman to win the Nobel Peace Prize said, "Nothing in life is to be feared, it is only to be understood." This leads to another common fear.

Fear of failure. Brenda remembers that same son, Vance, as she tucked him into bed, asking her for a prayer request. He said, "Mommy, will you pray that I can get my scissors and crayons into the right box and find my stuff." His was a summer birthday. His request and continuing anxiety over this simple task of scissors and crayons made her realize that maybe they had rushed Vance. He needed more time to develop before beginning kindergarten.

She checked with his teacher and his teacher had been concluding the same thing. He really needed a developmental year of kindergarten due to his late birthday and young age. That incident with her son made Brenda remember her own fear as she took tests at elementary school. Physically, her hands would get cold, and her forehead would get hot. Eventually, with continued practice, she outgrew that fear of test taking.

This is the second clue to helping a child overcome fear. Continual exposure in short intervals of test taking, with small successes helped calm irrational fears. In summary, slow, repeated patterns of success help a child to adjust to a new situation.

Of course, childhood fear of failure often accompanies us into adulthood. Brenda was talking to a very successful and admired man about his latest accomplishment. With a sheepish grin, he admitted that each morning when he was shaving, he looked into the mirror and said to himself, "Today may be the day that they find out." He wasn't sure that the adult man in the mirror was good enough or smart enough, despite his many achievements. He might just be found out and fall short. It was a mental irrational fear that lingered from childhood.

10

Fear of separation

Sometimes the first extended separation from family is sending the child to camp. Brenda found it to be different for each child. When Justin, her middle child, was eight, he said he reviewed two new things that summer. A burr haircut and camp. Next summer, he was going to go for the burr haircut only. He liked the minimal maintenance haircut. As far as camp—not so much.

He said night was hard and he would get homesick. His dad and mom dutifully wrote letters that arrived daily. He said getting letters only made it worse. He was glad to get home. Of course, before the car drive home ended, the newness had worn off and he was arguing with his brothers in the back seat. In the meantime, his brother Derek at 10 years was writing postcards. One read, "I pray for you every night. The chapel got wrecked by a boy named ___. One of the Ranger girls mooned us. Love Derek." He loved camp. When he later broke his collarbone at Boy Scout Camp, he refused the opportunity to leave camp early. He did not want to miss the fun.

Eileen, on the other hand, had a very independent daughter who had always been so. From Eileen: When we were living at West Point, a summer Bible camp was offered by our Chaplain, Father Fagan. We enrolled Brigid, then age 3. She knew Father Fagan, both from Church and from dinners with him in our home, so there was no worry about being "strange" or a case of separation anxiety.

On the second day of camp, Brigid walked into the kitchen at about 10:30 AM. Since camp had started at 8:30 AM, something was wrong. I asked her if Father Fagan had dropped her off. Her reply was, "No. I walked home." I was horrified. Mentally I reviewed that the chapel was ten blocks away, past derelict barracks, a muddy pond, and a steady stream of traffic.

I was standing there with my mouth open when the phone rang. It was a frantic Father Fagan trying to sound reassuring, saying that the Military Police were looking, and it wouldn't be long before they found Brigid. I told him that she was in the kitchen with me and asked for the M.P.'s to be called off, along with making an apology for my errant child.

"Why did you leave without telling an adult?" She looked at me as if I were the child and she the adult. "You see, the camp was very boring and there were always kids acting up. I did not want to hurt Father Fagan's feelings, so I left. It was the best idea." After a long lecture on acting responsibly and the need for being where you're supposed to be and not scaring Mommy by disappearing, we decided to end the Bible study for a while. The lesson for me was—don't let this kid be bored. It's one thing to encourage her independence and strong sense of self but another to scare the priest." Fear of separation it was not.

Another childhood common fear is a **fear of dogs**. In a survey, 37% of parents said their child was afraid of dogs even though a dog had not threatened or bitten their child. Brenda, too, had a fear of a certain type of dog, but it was created by a close encounter.

From Brenda: When I was in third grade and in Girl Scouts, we took turns bringing refreshments to the meeting. It was my turn. I had cupcakes and soft drinks in hand as I walked the few blocks to the home meeting. In those days soft drinks were in bottles. There was a loud clunking noise as the bottles rattled in the six pack of Dr. Pepper (of course, Dr. Pepper, remember, I am from Texas). You could certainly hear me coming. I rounded the corner and there, sitting in the front yard of a neighbor's home was a chow-chow.
This large orange dog with a huge mane immediately sprang to its feet. I cautiously proceeded to the far side of the street,

clunking and rattling. The chow was offended. It started across the street and close to me with a menacing growl which grew to nasty loud barking.

I froze in my tracks. It continued its approach and now was showing its teeth. It barked loud only inches away; I could feel its hot breath. I screamed and dropped the soft drink bottles as well as the cupcakes. Fortunately, another neighbor heard the commotion and yelled the dog's name. It answered his command to stop. I proceeded very shakily to the meeting. No refreshments made it. I never walked that way again, but, to this day, I have fears of a chow dog. His breath spoke as loud as his bark.

Eileen remembers: Until my adult years, I did not trust large dogs thanks to "Brownie." While visiting relatives in upper New York state, my cousin had a very large dog who was same height as the four-year-old me. I gleefully had a doughnut in my hand. Facing the dog, I sensed there was trouble. As a wily four-year-old, I quickly put the doughnut behind my back so Brownie would not get it. This did not fool Brownie. He jostled his way to getting that doughnut, leaving me both scared, less one doughnut, and disappointed with a distrust of large dogs for many years to come. It was only when as newlyweds, we got a harmless little puppy who grew to be the size of a small horse that I was able to tolerate a large dog. Later I came to appreciate his large size when our dog drove off a burglar from our apartment in Italy. He earlier had driven off a burglar in New York the night my husband had left for Viet Nam. That makes two for my sweet dog and zero for the burglars.

Once again, it helps a child to have careful and slow exposure of success. Small steps of success (and happy dog licks) help to gain trust and confidence that gives the right message to a child. It is ok to be scared but positive reinforcement of a successful experience can eventually overcome one unpleasant experience.

It is not only dogs that people fear. Eileen, as a city slicker from New York, considered both lizards and raccoons exotic and harmful animals. She said: I could not get my mail for two weeks because a lizard inhabited our mailbox. It had taken up permanent residence and would not leave. He seemed to enjoy taunting me. A later move to Savannah, Georgia, introduced a raccoon who liked to lurk outside our garage door. This interfered with doing the laundry. My non-sympathetic husband suggested I bang on a pan with a wooden spoon to alert the raccoon that I was opening the door. So, I, dutifully, never tried to sneak up on the raccoon and banged on a pan before doing the laundry for the next year. Eileen swears it was not a sweet looking Disney raccoon. It was a mothy, toothy, wrinkle- nosed scrawny raccoon. Fortunately, it did not need a hearing aid. Small successes **and** her laundry were accomplished.

Small successes help with another childhood fear. Another common fear for children is **lightning and thunderstorms**. There is a one in 700,000 chance of being struck by lightning, but the boom and flash are very scary to many children. When Brenda's sons were little, she wanted to make sure that they did not feel nervous. She said, "We would sit on the stairs so we could look out the front window from a safe distance in our Houston home. Texas gets some very crashing booms that rattle the house. We made it a game. When there was a flash, we would cheer and then count the seconds until the thunder boomed. It became a game rather than a threat. It also reflects that if the parent is not bothered by fear, then the child will reflect that confidence. The tip is to normalize the experience—my sons came to understand that thunder is normal, and lightning follows. It was a natural thing of beauty rather than scary."

Eileen agrees with this and tried to reflect the same calm when her young family moved to St. Louis. "Not being familiar with the difference between "alert" or "warning for a tornado," I saw the tornado symbol on the television. Not wanting to alarm my young daughter and son, I said, "Let's have a game of camping in the basement." I turned down the sound on the TV but kept an eye on the screen runner for the alert. Brigid and Brett pitched in with excitement over the gathering of pillows, sleeping bags, radio, food, etc. By this time, it was dark. My soldier husband was in Turkey and would not be home.

After several hours, there were no signs of the alert. I thought the children would be tired of the game. I really did not want to sleep in the basement, so I said, "Game over. Let us go to bed upstairs." But nooo. They were so disappointed. We all got to sleep in the basement that night."

On the other hand, Brenda did experience a damaging tornado in Houston, Texas. She was playing with her toddler in her bedroom while the other two young boys were napping upstairs. Glancing out her bedroom window, she saw something looping in the air and thought it was a bird. Then, she saw it wasn't a bird, but a roof shingle. She now could hear the approaching loud roar. Quickly, she scooped up her toddler Vance and pushed him safely inside a walk-in closet. Turning, she started running toward upstairs where the other two sons napped. Vance, of course, could not imagine why his mommy had put him in the closet so he toddled and cried after her.

Brenda looked at the open staircase. There was a two-story glass window behind the open stairs. She intuitively knew that the glass windows with a staircase were the weakest spot if a tornado hit. Her mind pictured trying to carry three children down the stairs. When the tornado hit, it would kill or bloody

15

them all. So, she turned back to carry the toddler to the closet and covered him with her body. All the while she listened to the freight train roar and the heaving of the roof which seemed to be pulling off its hinges. She prayed for protection. The threat was over within short but seemingly long minutes. After the heaving and pulling of the roof sounds stopped, she ran upstairs to check on her sons. Her young sons had napped through the whole noisy trauma.

The only resulting damage to the interior of the house was— the two-story window by the stairs. The window had indeed shattered, leaving glass covering the stairs. Her mental image had come true. On the outside, she saw the devastation of all the homes down the block to the east of her. Amazingly, the tornado had turned its path at her next-door neighbor's home. It spared Brenda's house. It had started at a diagonal angle which is the usual path of a tornado. This means it devastated the homes across the street and beyond.

Her home was like a standing oasis. The home honestly felt like guardian angels had taken the blows from the wind. Fortunately, there were no casualties in the neighborhood because most neighbors were not at home, but at work. However, there were many homes devastated to her right and across the street.
In facing this fear, Brenda knew what she had to do at the time of crisis, and she did it. And this is our third clue: she faced the fear with the help and support of a loving Father. She was on her knees with prayer. Our children need to know where our help comes from.

Another common fear for children is the **fear of heights**. Many of us can remember the taunts of "chicken on the high board." Eileen describes: 'Other friends dared me to jump from a high board at an indoor pool. Although not a strong swimmer, I took the dare. I climbed gingerly up the ladder, walked to the edge of the board and then, it happened. Tiny bumps of sweat made me inch backward down the board and down the ladder. I did not care if others mocked me; I wasn't going off the board. "More on Eileen's story later.

Brenda, too, suffers from those little bumps of sweat springing out on her palms and upper lip when she faces heights. Secretly she clutches the car door and quietly but firmly stomps on an imaginary brake on the passenger side while going down a mountain in a car. The driver may be exclaiming about the steep but gorgeous mountain view. Brenda is picturing Thelma and Louise. She knows it is irrational to think holding on to the door could help if the car went off the road, but somehow grasping the door makes this irrational fear go away.

There are other fears for children associated with health that occur. There is a **fear of blood.** When Brenda's husband needed blood and platelets for his fight with leukemia, in a show of support, her son's high school football team volunteered to donate blood. These healthy, strong football players lined up to donate blood. However, as is typical for blood donations, the hospital had to have a close watch for those who would faint. The attendants explained that at the sight of blood, the heart rate and blood pressure would rise for some donors. Then a sudden drop in pressure would lead to fainting, even for the strongest and bravest, but especially those with a big imagination. The young football team had both donations and big imaginations.

Taking this example further, even horror movies will play on the audience's fear of blood. Alfred Hitchcock played this fear very well. In his movie Psycho, he never shows a knife piercing the skin, but that Psycho shower scene has scared women for years, so that even today, some women shower with caution and look constantly over their shoulder in case a

Psycho is around. It is irrational fear, but it is there with our imagination.

Another common fear for children is **a fear of dentists or doctors**. Have you ever noticed a peculiar smell when you step into a dentist's office? An antiseptic minty scent seems to seep down the corridors into the waiting area. While your child or children squirm, you fill out page after page of forms to update what are supposed to be electronic forms. Somehow these hand- filled forms seem a contradiction in terms of electronics. Then, the favorite question lurks, "Does your child floss every day?"
 Does it count if you personally supervised that he flossed six times the day before your appointment? Even mothers fear the judgment of a dentist.

There is a saying, "If it is important to you, you will find a way. If not, you will find excuses." Or as Soupy Sales said, "Be true to your teeth and they will not be false to you." Again, the visits to the dentist or doctor often bring fear, but small successes in visits can overcome these normal childhood fears.

Let's Discuss

1. As a parent, we want to "fix" our children's fears. We want to intervene and manage the situation. Have you given the right message to your child and said it is ok to be scared? Have you tried the method of taking small successes slowly to fix a fear?

2. Have you shared how you also were afraid and shared a story with them so they can see that fear is normal and you had fears also? Have you had one of the previously mentioned childhood fears? What was it?

3. Have you talked to your child about a fear and have you been surprised that it was not the fear that you thought?

Some suggestions:

Have you tried to build their confidence by letting them control the situation? If there is a fear of the dark, night lights may help. My friend added lavender to water and put it in a spritzer bottle. The scent of lavender is calming, but the child is encouraged to spritz the monster with the spray and the monster will go "poof." She adds a funny story that says the monster is afraid of water and makes funny faces and gestures of how the monster can melt with the poof of a spray.

Have you tried teaching a child a phrase, like "I can do this!", or "Jesus loves me" as they face a fear? This should be repeated aloud and followed with a deep breath. While putting her children at ease before going to sleep, Brenda would sing "Jesus loves me." Often a baby voice would join her. Justin added his own version: "little children to him belong, they are weak, but I am strong!" Oh well, it was a model of being brave.

Have you helped them face their fears with faith and prayed with them and over them? We started the chapter with this verse: *"Don't worry about anything; instead, pray about everything. Tell God what you need and thank him for all he has done. Then you will experience God's peace, which exceeds anything we can understand. His peace will guard your hearts and minds as you live in Christ Jesus."* **Philippians 4:6-7**

Can you think of a time when you told God aloud what you needed, thanked him for all he has done and then felt the peace in your heart and mind?

How have you helped your child with their fear?

Chapter Three: Those Teen Years

He gives strength to the weary and increases the power of the weak. Even youths grow tired and weary and young men stumble and fall. But those who hope in the Lord will renew their strength. They will soar on wings like eagles, they will run and not grow weary, they will walk and not be faint." Isaiah 40: 29-31.

Even the young men stumble and fall. Childhood leads to the teen years. The teen years are full of fears and anxiety, so let's examine these fears.

One of the most profitable movies of all time is the Marvel Avenger series which is especially attractive to the teens. The heroes are clever, strong and defeat the bad guys. One of the most popular heroes is Thor, based on the Norse gods. He is strong, fast, and mostly smart. He comes from another place and intervenes just at the right time to pull people out of trouble. Too often, this is how teens imagine God. They see God as distant but hopefully popping up at the right time to save them from trouble. Then they grow into adults, depending on this same childish view—a distant but pop-up God.

This childish view of God is not very supportive as teens journey through the bumps of adolescence. At this point in their life, they need an all- present and all- beneficial God. Teens experience parental pressures to achieve, a trend toward overscheduling and sometimes too much involvement in video game violence.

Once again, fears of anxiety are fed by vivid imaginations. As children grow into their teenage years, these vivid imaginations contribute to social interaction fears. Teens make assumptions that feed their fears. Keeping pace with social media is the top of the list. With social media, their fear is that they won't be liked or appear to be unpopular. A typical teen reaction is if someone does not answer a text or dm quickly, the lack of quick response is taken that "the person doesn't like me or is mad at me." In today's internet forum where cowards hide, the chances of criticism or a negative post, or response is almost 100%.

Teens struggle so much with **the fear of disappointing others or the need to belong** that their hormonal blast could be described as "approval addicts." Professor Sherry Pagoto at the University of Massachusetts Medical School notes that "typically, the intense need to please and care for others is deeply rooted in either **a fear of rejection and/or fear of failure**. Fear of rejection is the underlying feeling that, 'if I don't do everything I can to make this person happy, they might leave or stop caring for me."

This tendency toward people pleasing is sometimes due to a lack of secure attachment in childhood that leaves a child anxious and yearning for more parental love and affirmation than he or she received.
From Brenda: My husband and I noticed when our eldest son reached puberty, his need to please his teenage friends

superseded his need to please us as parents. As a little tyke, he loved to put on a superman cape. It was not unusual for him to slip on his cape daily, strolling around the neighborhood to save the day. Consequently, as a teen, his friends and their approval became all important. He would stick out his neck to rescue or help a friend even at the risk of getting in trouble himself. As parents, we felt we no longer had boundaries that he would respect due to missed curfews, etc. We eventually talked with a counselor about "tough love." We were aware our son's fear resulted in regular attempts to win the approval and affection of other teens, even at his own risk of harm.

It was not an easy time for my son. As humans, we want to be liked, but "pleasers" have a higher-than-normal need for others to think well of them and to affirm them. We told the counselor very earnestly and sadly that sometimes we felt like we were throwing love down a bottomless pit. We just could not give enough love to fill that bottomless pit. The counselor's answer surprised us. He asked if our son were adopted. Yes, we nodded. He said that adopted kids often wear themselves out trying to help or rescue others. They are often prone to people pleasing, unwilling or unable to say no to others.

Research shows that all this activity to please others is about finding love and acceptance for us. Happily, my son as an adult has achieved adequate self-care and awareness so he is not as anxious and driven to people please. He is much more balanced. He believes it was until he was in his twenties to realize how deeply we loved him as parents. Coincidentally, he became a parent in his twenties. Often, teens do not understand a parent's love until they become a parent in their adult years.

Sometimes, as parents we must pray and wait it out. If you recognize in your teens that they or that you have a tendency

23

for obsessive people pleasing, Dr. Harriet Braiker's book, <u>The Disease to Please: Curing the People-Pleasing Syndrome</u> might prove helpful.

Another helpful insight is from Dr. Adam Hamilton in his book, <u>Unafraid</u>. Dr. Hamilton sums up people pleasing with: "Giving in to the fear of criticism practically guarantees that you will miss out on life and miss out on faithfully doing what God wants you to do. Jesus noted, 'Happy are you when people insult you and harass you and speak all kinds of bad and false things about you, all because of me. Be full of joy and be glad because you have a great reward in heaven.'" Matthew 5:11-12. As Adam Hamilton said, "When we finally trust in this grace offered by God, we stop trying to manipulate others into giving love and acceptance to us by our niceness. We have undeserved kindness from God who accepts us. Simply accept the fact that you are accepted. You have a heavenly parent who offers unconditional love. "

This reminded Eileen of a humiliating example to please the crowd. Earlier we mentioned her fear of heights on the high board. Eileen stated: "Some friends invited me on a ski trip. All was well. We stayed at a hotel with an indoor pool that shared a glass wall with the downstairs game room. The people in the game room could view the swimmers from an underwater vantage point. This small group of friends casually divided into two groups. Some chose the game room; others chose swimming in the pool. One of the swimmers suggested we all dive in and wave to our friends in the game room. I was not a strong swimmer.

Not to be outdone, I decided I could do it! I bravely made a dive and with a surge pushed straight into the bottom of the pool. This caught their attention! Feeling good and like a swimming star, with another strong surge I dramatically pushed upward to the surface. To add to my crowning touch, I lifted my arms with a flourish to wave. Too late I realized my swimsuit top had popped loose and stayed down while I was energetically waving upwards. My sudden realization caused a huge inward gasp. I sucked in water. Now I was practically drowning in embarrassment and water. When I got to the top and was able to breathe, I rasped, "Please throw me a towel." Slowly, slowly my bathing suit top floated to the surface. The desire was to drown quietly. I knew I was being watched. I escaped to my room. This was never mentioned again by the viewers. But I knew, they knew."

Brenda told her eldest son that she always prayed that if he were with a group and doing something wrong, that he would get caught. Her hope was that by being caught, it would prevent him from proceeding to a further, worse consequence. He said in a surprised voice, "So that's why I always seemed to get caught and others didn't!"

He did not forget what she said. A few years ago, she admitted to him that after years of never getting a traffic ticket, she had recently gotten three speeding tickets in three months. With a smile, he said, "Yes. I have prayed for you, that if you are doing something wrong, you'd get caught." Hmm. Sometimes they do listen.

This two-way listening is key for helping our teens. Sometimes they have fears long before we are aware. Eileen remembers: On the first day of kindergarten, as the parents and grandparents waited with their kindergarteners to enter the class, one child sobbed uncontrollably and held on to his mother's leg. The teacher kindly told the mother to just wait it out and they would have cookies and milk shortly and she could leave. As the child was consoled with cookies and milk, my granddaughter approached him. With a soft voice, she said, "I think you might be my date for the senior prom." The boy just kept stuffing the cookies. Eileen had no idea of where a senior prom played any interest for her granddaughter or a kindergarten boy. I think that kid remembers it because to this day, he is a little wary of the interest of my granddaughter.

It seems that a vast number of fear-based decisions are long in the making. College fears may start early. Teens fear making the grade on SAT, or being accepted in the "right" university, or getting scholarships to help defray cost. Fears surround them on selecting a college, not only financially but also in separation anxiety. A teen's reluctance to choose a long-distance college may be a sign that they fear traveling so far away from home. They are not developmentally ready for separation.

Parental enthusiasm or dreams of their future should not overrun what the teen is ready for. To have a non-judgmental two-way conversation is very hard. As a parent, Brenda admits she wanted college for all three sons. It was the burst of a bubble to find out her eldest son wasn't really interested in college at all. He was sick of school and preferred to go to Colorado to get a technical certificate which he eventually never used. Some students choose a gap year which may turn out to be very productive in some cases. Some parents fear that this gap will distract, rather than focus their teen. As it turns out, Brenda's oldest son still feels that he made the right choice of no college as he is very entrepreneurial and has initiated several business ventures. Colorado is where he met his future wife. But, on the other hand, he values the professional advice of his brothers who also would not change their decisions to gain MBAs.

Admittedly, in dealing with the fears of teens, monosyllables from them dot most conversations. The hardest frustration is trying to have a two-way discussion in a non- judgmental way. But this two-way conversation is the only way that the fears beneath the teen decisions can surface. Otherwise, as parents, we make assumptions that may be far from the truth. We tell ourselves stories and reasonings that are our own assumptions.

Let's Discuss:

1. Teens struggle so much with the fear of disappointing others or with the need to belong that their hormonal blast could be described as approval addicts. Have you experienced this need to belong or observed an excessive need to belong in your teenager(s)?

2. Have you noticed your own tendency to people pleasing? Can you think of times when you have tried to manipulate others by your niceness? Could you describe some examples of someone being an approval addict?

3. Can you remember some teenage fears that you experienced, or can you name some fears that your own children experience?

4. Have you shared this verse with a loved one: *He gives strength to the weary and increases the power of the*

weak. Even youths grow tired and weary and young men stumble and fall. But those who hope in the Lord will renew their strength. They will soar on wings like eagles, they will run and not grow weary, they will walk and not be faint." Isaiah 40: 29-31.

5. What does that verse mean to you? Have you experienced that those who hope in the Lord will renew their strength? You cannot change yourself. That extreme power only comes from God. But the Bible tells us that when you put your trust in Him, it opens to eternity so that your change of heart is forever.

6. Do you limit God to a Marvel comic Thor, who pops in to save you and has human limitations? Do you believe in a God that is all powerful with nothing too big for Him to accomplish? God who created the universe is throughout creation and can rewire and inspire you. Are you spending time getting to know this God or are you keeping the Thor version?

Chapter Four: Bullying and Splat! There goes grape jelly

We cannot talk about the fears of teens or parenting without examining the phenomenon of bullying. Feeling alone and isolated has taken epic proportions in the United States, especially among teens. Consequently, irrational fear often takes the form of Bullying.

Bullying is not limited to schools, but also cyberspace and the workplace. To feel better about themselves, there are those who will try to make a scapegoat of someone else. Unfortunately, bullies do not get the idea that blowing out someone's candle does not make yours shine brighter. In a 2019 survey, 79% of the males and 83% of the females reported that they had been bullied in school.

From Brenda: I am sitting in Mrs. Sheridan's office waiting to hear the disciplinary action of an "infraction" where my seventh-grade son had shouted an obscenity at a group, publicly repeating obscenities that had been said to him by another boy earlier in the day. I recognize that he is at the boiling point, feeling harassed by others and humiliated. I sit staring at the worn green carpet where it meets the line of concrete in the hall. The aroma of warm rolls baking for lunch in the cafeteria conflicts with the odor of slightly stinky antiseptic mops. It is Middle School, and I am waiting for the principal.

Middle school is tough on all the kids. With hormones racing, kids look for scapegoats. Attacking in person or in cyberspace, their taunts seem magnified. The ADD child is a frequent target. Easily aroused to anger or tears, tolerance seems frazzled or worn to nothing. Praise for the ADD child is a necessary ingredient, but it must be for small wins, not waiting for major victories. Punishment is much easier.

Attention Deficit Disorder was diagnosed for Brenda's eldest son and for 3-10% of teens at that time in 1988. By 2023, the number of diagnoses has increased 42%. It crosses racial, ethnic, and social lines. It causes dropouts and more importantly suicides or juvenile delinquency run-ins. Suicides happen because being a target of bullying has become too much of a burden.

The impulsiveness of ADD sets up kids as a victim because it relieves other kids from being in the hot seat. "Group think" will select a favorite victim. If the heat is off, the ADD kid often will jump back into the fire with a fast remark or an impulsive action. Unfortunately, this type of kid has too thin a filter to let taunts roll off. In the meantime, they do not filter their own impulsive behavior.

It becomes a handicap that makes the student work twice as hard to show "normal" productivity. Scrawled handwriting camouflages good thoughts. Disorganization loses good homework. Lack of focus wastes class time. Hearing only one half of the verbal instructions, their brain cannot filter the noise around them. Copying passages from the board onto paper makes double demands of laborious fine motor skills that fatigue the brain. Sitting upright on a spine rather than in a reclined slouching position often blocks the circulation flow. That is why the ADD child often prefers sitting angularly on the floor.

Is the child lazy, unmotivated, and assertive? Or is the child worn thin by "forgetting" medication, resulting in the aggravation of peers and teachers by their "acting out behavior"? If a child were blind, would he be handed a printed book? If he wore an outward leg brace, would the same standards be held for him to run as well as other children? Is ADD an inward handicap that causes outward impulsive behavior? The educational system sometimes allows for the symptoms, but bullies often make this impulsive behavior a favorite target for their bullying.

Brenda questions the fears that arise from ADD and bullying. She questions as a parent, did we have tough love and let him suffer the consequences? Or did we try to make allowances with strong boundaries? Did we expect too much? Was the bar too high? Or were we enabling poor judgment by making excuses? Were we helicopter parents, hovering too much? Was suicide a very real possibility in dark impulsive moments? It was a question that we never quite came up with an answer. But it took up a great deal of our parenting time dealing with bullies and impulsive actions of our son. This, too, affected the family as a system. Brenda worried about the ripple effect on the observing siblings. Were they victimized by residual effects?

Eileen states, "Bullying takes many forms. Child to child, adult to adult or it can be teacher to child, teacher to parent or parent to teacher. "The burden of hyperactivity can be passed from parent to child. My husband Joe wasn't every teacher's dream. He got into trouble a lot. The Baby Boomers of Long Island were so numerous that it was common for elementary class sizes to range from 45-60 children. For many teachers it was more important to maintain order than to engage young minds. It was a case where smart kids finished assignments quickly leaving lots of time and opportunity to screw up. Who knows, even ADD, a condition not yet discovered at that time, was the cause for my husband Joe's behavior. In any case, Joe spent a lot of time in time outs.

The situation continued into high school where his teachers were Brothers of the Holy Cross. Imagine our surprise when we found that those same religious Brothers would be teaching our children in Rome at the Notre Dame International School. Founded following World War II, it continued serving the English-speaking community. Children had to be interviewed to be accepted with both parents present. So it was that the four of us arrived at the school, well- scrubbed, nicely dressed and with great expectations.

We met at the door and were escorted to the admissions office. The Brother in charge walked in after a few minutes. He stopped in his tracks and stared at Joe. Then his glare transferred to our son. He paused and directing his words to our son, he said, "If you're anything like your father, you're going to be in big trouble here." Yep, this Brother was one of the many who disciplined Joe back in High School. Clearly this Brother had an amazing memory. Just as clearly, Joe had made a lasting impression and not a good one.

Getting off on the wrong foot happens to us all. What we do about it is what makes the difference. In Brett's case, it led to good behavior. Very good behavior at that school. He knew he was being watched.

Now we need to fast forward seven years. Since I had been teaching for several years, by the time my son entered high school, I knew the politically correct way to speak "Teacherese." For example, I could hear, "your son is very verbal." Yes, he could not shut up. Or "your son thinks out of the box. Yes, he'd finish what was required and then get into trouble doing something else—not educationally related-- while the other students finish. Sometimes he was the instigator of disruption. Many of the things that had plagued his father were the same behaviors that now plagued the son.

The teacher called a meeting. She was a sweet young thing, teaching French her first year out of college. I knew she did not want to offend me by telling me about my son's unruly behavior in her class. She simply wanted him gone—even to an elective class in Under Water Basket Weaving—but gone to another class. Unfortunately, that solution would wreck his schedule. For one class, he would have to change his entire schedule of seven other classes with the semester half gone. He was doing well in his other classes. There had to be another way. Unfortunately, the bullying tactic became her mode.

We sat opposite each other. She fully expected us to do what she told us. She did not consider it a dialogue. She straightened in her chair. She had called the meeting. She had the solution. How did we have the nerve to push back or make it a two-way conversation?

As I met her stare, I realized she was trying the bully tactic. She wanted him gone. I thought to myself, why does a person bully? It means she is insecure—as a teacher, as a person in authority. So how does one handle a bully? In this case, how does one make it a win/win situation?

I was not fooled. I knew that my son could be a culprit in disruption once he had finished his work. But part of being a good teacher is to challenge the students at all levels to move a class forward. As parents, we did not accept bad behavior on our son's part because it meant a lack of respect. I considered it a teaching moment for all of us—parent, child, new teacher. She considered it a challenge to her authority. At that point, the only thing she wanted to talk about was his behavior and that she wanted him gone. We were at an impasse.

As a teacher, I had been bullied by parents who thought their child could do no wrong. I was not excusing my child. In dealing with a bully in conflict, I knew we had to seek a common goal. What did we both want? We both wanted to lessen the tension and concentrate on the academics. He was achieving good test scores, with pitch perfect pronunciation. Based on the time remaining in the term his cooperation was the key. As parents, we proposed that he should be punished for any infraction of the class rules. Further, we would monitor his assignments and stay in communication with her until the end of the semester. We also promised he would drop French at the end of the semester. But we wanted him to stay in the class until the end of the term.

Fortunately, the lack of fluency in French has not been a deterrent in Brett's life. Besides completing law school, he is multi-lingual, speaking Italian, Arabic and some Spanish having served in the Peace Corps. It might not have been a win/win situation, but at least we were not bullied into a win/lose.

Sometimes defending another against a bully can also get you in trouble. When our daughter Brigid was a sophomore in high school, she saw a bully taunting another girl at the required swimming class. This female (Big Mac supersized) was six inches taller and at least 60 pounds heavier than Brigid. For the past few lessons, the bully had targeted a small girl threatening to throw her in the water and drown her. The girl was terrified of the water and the bully enjoyed pushing her into the pool. Brigid saw this and decided on her own that she needed to do something. Brigid stepped between the bully and the girl when it happened again and said to stop. The bully's response was what are you going to do about it? Brigid's answer was to ball up her fist and cold cock the girl.

We were called to the principal's office and listened in disbelief that our heretofore mild-mannered child had hit someone and was going to be suspended. When I asked where the bully was, I was told she had been sent home and would not be receiving disciplinary action. I asked if the bully had ever gotten into trouble in the school before. There was a pregnant pause, clearing the throat, looking at the ground, but no response. I said I did not think it was right for only one person to be suspended when upon further investigation it was seen that she was defending another girl who had been threatened on several occasions with drowning. While we would never encourage violence, we were secretly proud of the fact that she had placed her safety aside as she stood up to this bigger girl. However, we did agree that she should be suspended. But we also believed the other girl should be suspended. As it turns out, the bully never returned and to our chagrin we discovered the physical education teacher for whatever reason had known of the situation and did nothing. When we talked to Brigid about the use of violence, she shook her head and said, "But Mom, the next time she might die."

Consequently, Eileen and Brenda have a suggestion for handling verbal bullying. When bullying, power playing or criticism in the workplace or at school occurs, it is often an irrational fear on one or the other's part. We are not talking about physical fear. Physical bullying needs other action to be taken. Here is a suggestion to handle **verbal bullying**:

We call this the hula hoop perspective. Imagine that you have a hula hoop around your waist. Within the hula hoop is my business, my self-confidence, and my personal space. Someone can be allowed in only by invitation. On the outside of the hula hoop is my invisible protective shield. I can let the world toss opinions, judgment, and perceptions at me. I can let these fly at me, splat onto the protective shield and just like grape jelly, watch it slowly drift down the protective shield.

I can and should examine it. I can decide if it is true or not true and then take or leave the statements. But I don't have to let it get inside my hula hoop and take it personally unless I have judged it to be valid.
It is hard even as an adult, not to take something personally. We let it get to us. It sneaks inside our shield. We go over and over it in our minds. If we can recognize that it was tossed by an insecure bully who has fears of his or her own, we can "shake it off." There goes grape jelly!

This is especially hard in the vulnerable teen years. We let others define our reality and perception of self. Anonymous bullies on the internet toss these opinions, judgment, and perceptions onto our hula hoop. Therefore, we need to let it splat. We need to consider the source, watch it roll off the shield and decide if it has any truth or value. It may just be irrational taunts.

Brenda remembers her Middle School experience with bullying from the very girls she thought were her friends. Brenda says: A critical handwritten note awaited me on my desk when I returned happily from being recognized for a school award. It was signed by a dozen or so of my classmates who would have liked to receive that same award. My friends stated they no longer wanted to be my friend. Was it truth, bullying or jealousy?

After major agonizing tears when I got home that afternoon and night, I began, even at that tender age, to realize it for what it was. One girl had initiated the note and bullied my friends into signing a note that criticized me as no longer a friend simply because I had gotten an honor that she wanted. She was not a happy person. In fact, she remained a bully through high school. I knew it; I could figure it out. But it did not make it feel better. That's when I knew. I had to shake it off. . .and find new friends. There goes grape jelly!

Who among us has not been the victim of Mean-Spirited people? With group chats and the internet, comments are made from cowards who would never say those comments in person. Perhaps our national mantra to stop bullying should be "there goes grape jelly." This is a two-way street.

* Feedback from a good friend is a gift and should be valued.

* I need to analyze the feedback like grape jelly—is it valid?

*After analyzing the splat, allow the rest of the criticism to roll off the protective shield of the hula hoop like grape jelly— slow, painfully messy and sticky, but not something for us to allow inside.

* When I give feedback, am I being Analytical or is it Critical because I covet? What is my motive when I give feedback to others? Am I jealous of what they have?

Finally, when dealing with a bully and feeling overwhelmed by an irrational fear (not a physical one), we need to remember that we have support. It is that third clue again.

An example is in the Old Testament. Elijah was a man of God. However, when word reached him, that Queen Jezebel had threatened his life, like most of us, he took the easy option. He ran (1 Kings chapter 19). Also, Elijah prayed and complained about how he was being treated. The Lord's answer: " *And, behold, the Lord passed by, and a great and strong wind rent the mountains, and broke in pieces the rocks before the Lord; but the Lord was not in the wind: and after the wind an earthquake; but the Lord was not in the earthquake: And after the earthquake a fire; but the Lord was not in the fire: and after the fire a still small voice"*

What Elijah thought was not true. The story he told himself was not true. Elijah thought God was silent and that Elijah was the only one left. God was not only "not silent," but He had an army of angels waiting and surrounding him. Elijah was not alone in this Wilderness experience, but the answer was not in a powerful roar. It was in a still small voice.

Therefore, when God seems silent, it may mean that we have stopped listening. We have no idea of the abundance of help just outside the door. We have allowed the cares of this world to plug our spiritual ears. God does not usually speak to us today in signs of fire or wind. His Spirit speaks to us through the Word in a still small voice. It blocks out the voice of the insecure, false bullies of this world who do not deserve for us to listen. Splat! There goes grape jelly!

What do you think? Let's Discuss:

1. Bullying is a national phenomenon. Do you remember being bullied? Describe it.

2. Are we caught in a victim syndrome where we create villains? By making **other** people the villains and making excuses, this allows us to remain helpless. Are we allowing ourselves to remain stuck in victim syndrome?
If we take control and *not act like a victim*, does it make the road out of the wilderness shorter?

3. Have you experienced getting it all wrong or realizing it was not what you originally thought? What story did you tell yourself?

Chapter Five: Marriage Fears

Marriage is a great institution. I'm not ready for an institution yet. Mae West

It has been asked, what is the difference between love and marriage. The humorous answer is "Love is blind. Marriage is an eye opener!" There are fears we all have about marriage. Let's discuss!

Fears include emulating your parent's marriage, not being accepted by your spouse's family, rocking the boat, loss of independence, and being rejected or alone. As we approach marriage from diverse experiences, one of the most common fears is **emulating your parent's marriage**.

Eileen says, "I didn't want the marriage of my parents because they had stagnated with lives stuck in concrete. They were mild mannered, painstakingly careful. It was the Love Song of J Alfred Prufrock. They didn't try new things or go new places but complacently lived a day-to-day life that appeared monotonous to me. It seemed their goal was to get to Friday night. Everyone in the family lived within a half mile in New

York. No one moved beyond family boundaries. I knew I never wanted to be an image of them. They coped but did not thrive.

Joe and I wanted their ethics: loyalty, trust and respect of marriage but also to have adventure. By marrying my husband on the eve of his going to Viet Nam, I knew we would both try new vistas. And it was not plain Vanilla. On my husband's side, his parents' NYC marriage appeared to me to be based on image. Images were where they went to a restaurant, the clothes they wore, the vacations in Breezy Point, the cruises and the people they hung out with. Image can be awfully limiting. My mother-in-law was the perfect Corporate wife: selecting his clothes, giving dinner parties, and making him feel pampered with his favorite cocktail in her hand when he came in the door."

As "people pleasers" many daughters-in-law suffer in adjusting to trying to meet the approval of their mother-in-law. Many daughters-in-law have a **fear of not being accepted** by the mother-in-law or the spouse's family. Many times, being accepted or loved is never achievable. Eileen believed that her role model was her mother-in-law. If she could achieve her mother-in-law's social skills of interacting with all types of people, entertaining every level of society with ease, always looking well dressed and well coifed, and always very self-confident, she would meet with her mother-in-law's approval. On the other hand, her mother-in-law was hugely protective of her family, never wanting her son or husband to appear in a bad light. It was almost as if no one could ever be good enough to marry her son. Does this sound familiar to you?

As a people pleaser, Eileen never gave up. Eileen wanted to be the daughter her mother-in-law never had. However, her mother-in-law wasn't receptive to expanding her family. Approval took a very long time to finally be accomplished.

On the other hand, Brenda's mother-in-law gave full approval from the first. At Brenda's wedding, Leta said, "I am giving my son to you." With a laugh, she then said, "Don't give him back." Brenda said, "She always supported me as if I were a prize. Of course, she couldn't understand why I didn't excel or even try to be the excellent seamstress and good cook that she was. Her priorities were not my strengths. My lack of skill or lack of interest in sewing or cooking puzzled her. She brought it up often with little subtle gifts of sewing utensils or cookbooks. Eventually she gave up on my cooking or sewing abilities."

Brenda, too, had interesting role models for marriage. This was the **fear of rocking the boat or confrontation**. For Brenda's parents, their loving encompassed "if Mama's happy, everyone's happy." Mother was a fragile Steel Magnolia, the adult child of an alcoholic. Rocking the boat wasn't what anyone in the family was inclined to do--neither husband nor two daughters rocked the boat. Brenda and her sister never really got into teen age rebellion despite strict rules. This didn't mean sharp arguments did not occur. Arguments might abound, but as Brenda's dad said, "You'll never change her mind. Just go with the flow." He operated in passive resistance. It was a lesson that Brenda and her sister learned early. So, the family and her parent's marriage were relatively happy for their 56 years of marriage. No one rocked the boat.

On the other hand, Brenda's husband 's parents had the **older man/younger wife syndrome**. He was a successful Company Man with a law degree to boot. He married late and had children when he was almost forty. He married a wife ten years younger. He tended to be grumpy. She tended to be flighty. She would laugh to say that he was not handsome, but he was a sought-after bachelor. She did all the right things for him, but she undermined her position by being flighty. She certainly undermined his disposition. However, all four sets of parents for Eileen and Brenda's families had 50 plus years of 'until death we do part marriages.' All four sets would be classified as good parents with acceptable marriages.

That was then and this is now.

Neither Eileen nor Brenda emulated their parents' marriage. The walk down the aisle for both Brenda and Eileen fifty years later did not turn out as either imagined. The marriage of fifty years ago does not look the same in partnership or style. Fifty years ago, it would be the solo bread winner who determined where the family would live. If Eileen followed her parents' pattern, she, too, would return to life in Bayside, New York. Having seen most parts of the world, Joe and Eileen have never felt the desire to go back to Bayside. Their satisfying partnership has not relived the less than satisfying model of either of their parents. Furthermore, neither Joe and Eileen nor Brenda and David stayed in the profession that they each graduated from college with.

 None of the certainties that were pictured when they first married have evolved. After world- wide travel, Joe and Eileen have settled to a farm in Connecticut. Brenda was widowed from a happy marriage of thirty-three years. A short "snickers" marriage occurred later down the road. She calls it a Snickers marriage. It was short and momentarily satisfying, but not a healthy choice. Since then, singlehood has been the role that Brenda would not have imagined in her youth.

Modern marriage looks different today. What is the new normal? Historian Stephanie Coontz says that "til death do us part" has taken a dive. Divorce rates are declining for people in their prime child-rearing years but doubling for people over fifty and *tripling* for people over sixty-five. After children leave, current mortality rates indicate we have thirty more years of healthy life. Some people realize they don't want to spend those years with their current partner. Coontz maintains that the automatic advantage of getting married has declined and miserable marriages are a health risk. However, the advantages of a good marriage are increasing. When marriages are working, they improve women's health and wealth.

Our lives have also changed in terms of work and geographical locations. Some women, at one time, have feared a **loss of independence**. However, even though married, you may face geographic separation as you both pursue a fulfilling career. This is becoming more of a current situation for millennials. For example, Eileen's daughter Brigid worked for a year in another country from her husband. Brigid by choice had pursued an excellent job in Bermuda, while her husband fought fires in the States. Decades ago, the husband's job had priority and determined where the family lived. Now, the wife may be the larger breadwinner. Furthermore, a family must consider when accepting a job, that it may not turn out to be the right job. There needs to be a trial period before uprooting the entire family. Or, either of the breadwinners can be laid off unexpectedly and find the family limited to one paycheck, going from two family income to one which won't pay the bills. In Brigid's case, her husband is a firefighter in Connecticut which took many years and certifications to achieve. Since her job took her to Bermuda, he found ways to swap time on the job with another firefighter whose wife had taken a job in California. In doing so, both husbands could spend one month in the States and a few weeks in Bermuda or California to join their family. Both families made separation work. Now, Brigid has mirrored her husband's work by getting a Ph.D. specializing in counseling for PTSD (post traumatic syndrome) for fire fighters and police.

This phenomenon of dual countries is not new in Europe. When Brenda did a consulting stint in Lithuania, she found most women in the Lithuanian workforce had learned English quickly. After the Russians left Lithuania, the new employment language became English. The women transitioned into employment much faster than the men who still spoke Russian and couldn't find employment. It was common for the men to go to a nearby country where the economy was better. Thus, in Lithuania it may be a dual income, dual **country** family.

In today's marriage, consequently, there has been another evolvement. It is not obvious who earns the higher salary. In contrast, when Eileen and Brenda were brides in the 70's, a wife's occupation typically ended at the altar. It was expected that the wife would quit her job to have children and to contribute to her husband's career in a support mode. The occupations of teaching and nursing were acceptable to continue briefly, but typically were abandoned once children arrived. Men often did not like for their wife to work because they feared it would appear they could not support the family. Only one third of all women were in the workforce. By the 1990's the phenomenon of "dincs" or dual income families became more common. The husband of today takes a much more active role in childcare due to dual income responsibilities. Often it is the husband who takes off work to take the ill child to the doctor. Millennials have improved the percentages of both parents taking an active role in parenting. Since women can earn a successful living, they can be partnered by choice rather than by necessity. Marriage has evolved.

But marriage remains hard work. As Shauna Niequist points out in "Present over Perfect", the new normal in evolved marriages still "allows men to eat when they're hungry, sleep when they're tired, run when they're antsy and leave when they're ready to leave. But even the most driven, articulate, strong women I know struggle to really meet their own needs. . .when really that cherished (do it all) reputation keeps me tangled up, needs unmet, voice silenced?" We are evolving, but the **fear of imperfection** nags on.

Another common fear for marriage is **commitment**. Brenda remembers saying as a young girl, "what if I decide to get married and someone comes along that I like better." According to the role models and mindset of the time, there was rarely such thing as a "do over." Later, as a mature adult, entering her second marriage following her widowhood, there was a fear of commitment due to a worry of what if I don't love him enough, or what if I am settling and rushing into this commitment. With marriage, we are risking our hearts and allowing someone into our innermost private space.

Fear of commitment is followed by a fear of **rejection or a fear of loss** in a marriage. Psychologists will tell that this fear of loss or rejection is the most basic fear of all. People **fear being alone**. As humans, we are trying to find our person, and we desperately want to be equally cherished by and not to lose our person.

We like to be alone, but we hate to be lonely. The actress Jodie Foster has described this well, "It's an interesting combination. Having a great fear of being alone yet having a desperate need for solitude and the solitary experience, that's always been a tug of war for me."

Therefore, how do we face these typical fears in marriage?

The need for a relationship has been a part of human nature since the beginning of time. God saw that Adam was lonely and He created Eve. Later in Genesis 2:24 *"Therefore a man leaves his father and his mother and clings to his wife, and they become one flesh."*

We look for keys to having a happy, fulfilling, life-long experience if we choose marriage rather than singlehood. We desperately want to be equally yoked and happy. Here is a thought suggested by the Bible.

Marriage is a covenant between two people and God. Keeping God as part of the covenant and marriage is the key to success. Children are part of the temporary assignment of the covenant, but marriage is a promise. It requires one long ongoing and vital conversation. It needs to be a two-way conversation. It cannot be placed on auto pilot. How easily we drift into auto pilot.

Marriage is often begun due to chemistry. We pursue each other, we look good and act our best. Then, once we have made the covenant, do we stop the pursuit and get lazy? Think about it. If we get lazy with our career, our body, our landscaped yard, will it improve on its own or decrease through lack of attention? Have we looked in the mirror lately? The same happens to marriage if we get lazy.

Sometimes we act like our marriage is a contract rather than a covenant.

A contract is an agreement dependent upon the performance of the two parties—I'll keep my end of the bargain if you keep yours. A covenant is sacred with "all I have and all I am are yours." Have we devolved into the attitude of a contract? "Now that we're married, you are supposed to take out the trash, or cook the meals or take care of the children. That's just your job." We take it for granted that these things will get done, because the other is "supposed to." A covenant means being appreciative of the hard work that a marriage takes. The question is whether you are intentionally holding up your end of the covenant with gratitude for the others in the covenant. Or even more imbalanced, is when you are leaving God out of the relationship.

God does give help to a marriage. In the first place, Jesus has entered the covenant in Hebrews 13:5, *"I will never leave nor forsake you."* But in 1 Corinthians 13:4-7 is a list that all of us must work on in a marriage. (Many people use these verses in wedding ceremonies. The tough part is following up with the concepts when the honeymoon is over.) *"Love is patient, love is kind. It does not envy, it does not boast, it is not proud. It is not rude; it is not self-seeking. It is not easily angered; it keeps no record of wrongs. Love does not delight in evil but rejoices with the truth. It always protects, always trusts, always hopes, always perseveres."*

Therefore, the follow-up of help is that patience is creating space, not pressure. Love is considering the other person's feelings. It is not one upping in a contractual agreement. It is slow to anger and not keeping tabs of who did what. Basically, it is trusting, hoping, and filling the other person's love tank. If their tank runs dry, they don't have much fuel or energy to give back to the relationship.

The only spouse you can change is your spouse's spouse.

It is tough work to practice this 1 Corinthians list. It must be intentional to model the person that you want your partner to be. A picture is worth 1000 words.

If we are modeling this picture, with the help of God, then the fear of a stifled marriage, lack of commitment and rejection can dissipate. It turns into trust, hope and perseverance.

Counselors have stated that if you model the picture of what you want your spouse to be by being it yourself for 60 days, the marriage will change. Or at least your spouse's spouse will have changed. Is it time to Redesign or Decline?

Let's Discuss:

1. Have you experienced the fear of emulating your parent's marriage? What would you like to avoid? What would you like to keep?

2. Have you experienced the fear of commitment? What is holding you back? Have you experienced the fear of loss or rejection? How has that affected your relationships?

3. Do you struggle with the fear of loneliness and the need for solitude? How have you found a balance?

4. *"And pray in the Spirit on all occasions with all kinds of prayers and requests. With this in mind, be alert and always keep on praying for all the Lord's people."* Ephesians 6:18. Have you applied this verse to your marriage? How has prayer given you a sense of gratitude for the strengths in your partner or the ability to accept the weaknesses in your partner or loved ones? How about praying for your weaknesses? You take on the whole enchilada, not just the parts you like.

Chapter Six: Motherhood/Parenting Fears: Soaring or Sinking

God put me on this Earth to accomplish a certain number of things. Right now, I am so far behind I will never die. ~ Bill Watterson

Or try this wardrobe on for size:
"As God's chosen ones, holy and beloved, clothe yourselves with compassion, kindness, humility, meekness and patience . . .Above all, clothe yourselves with love, which binds everything together in harmony." Colossians 3:12-14

We have discussed the Fears that abound in childhood and the Fears that come with marriage. Next there are fears and frustrations that come with Parenting. We would all enjoy a "how to" manual to accompany the birth of each child. Parenting brings fears.

From Brenda: David and I adopted our first child. We brought Derek home from the hospital when he was three days old. I stared at him on the hour's drive home, hardly able to believe that he was now my beautiful child. He weighed six and a half pounds, was perfectly formed and naturally was beautiful. He was everything we had hoped for and more. He was calm and slept a lot. As new parents, we were not—either calm or sleepy. That first night we set the alarm for 2 AM so we could check on him. We peered into the crib to see a perfectly happy and sleeping baby. "But isn't he hungry?" we whispered to each other. "Shouldn't he have awakened by now. . . Is something wrong?"

Yes. We did it.

We woke up a perfectly sleeping baby to feed him, fearful that maybe he needed food and would die of hunger.

Of course, in later days we grew to realize that he was a normal baby and would let us know, loud and clear, when he was ready. We got in his rhythm of a practical feeding schedule. Not for the first time, I realized that maybe it was not a fear issue but a faith issue. I needed to fear less and trust more in God's natural order and motherhood."

Brenda also remembers checking "child development books" chapter by the chapter with her first son. She says, by the third son, I let *him* read to *me* in baby chatter with an upside-down book, sitting in my lap. Vance was happy to pretend. I was just happy to sit down. Another thrill was to get to take a shower without the shower door being yanked open for me to settle an argument (or to referee a "discussion.") I still remember staring down at a three-foot stranger who had yanked open my shower door. It was a neighbor's kid who was part of the gang, but I had not met. He felt he needed a referee with my sons while I was soaping up and naked in the shower. Fortunately, he was only 4 years old, and the argument was not large.

One of the biggest fears as you get pregnant is the **fear of abnormalities of your future baby**. Eileen remembered going home from an appointment and talking out loud to her baby that it would be okay.

Eileen said: I had chicken pox in the first trimester of pregnancy. The local general practitioner said it would not be a problem. When I told my regular doctor, what a relief it was that there would not be complications since I had chicken pox, all conversation stopped. He left the room. When he came back into the room, he offered an abortion. On the way home from the doctor, I talked to my baby and said it was going to be okay. And it was. When I came out of delivery from a healthy baby boy, I fearfully wanted to look because I thought he had a harelip. I wasn't wearing glasses." As it turns out, Eileen says he was a healthy baby, but he did not have immunity to chicken pox. He later contracted chicken pox not once but four times after the age of three.

If you have never experienced pregnancy, you do not really know what to expect. Typical questions that occur to a mother-to-be represent multiple fears:

Will I be competent and meet my child's needs because my own mother did/or didn't?
Will I lose my identity in my profession or as a wife?
Will I be able to balance my work, professional and personal life?
Will I still be desirable to my husband, and will my looks change?

These fears affect the fluctuating self-confidence and self-image of a young parent. Once the baby has arrived, let's examine these fears that parents face.

Eileen remembers that the birth of the second child reinforced a fear of **lack of control**. When her first child, Brigid, had

Hemophilus influenza at three years, Joe and Eileen were at West Point. Brigid kept complaining of a sore throat. Eileen took her to the Emergency room at West Point. Even though she had swollen glands, the doctor told Eileen to go home and give her aspirin. She went home. A few hours later Brigid's glands had swollen so that she was having to hold her chin upwards to breathe.

Eileen drove quickly through the night to get her daughter back to the emergency room. When she arrived, Brigid's three-year-old neck had swollen to about 27 inches. This time, the orderlies took her out of Eileen's arms and put her on a gurney. Over his shoulder, the doctor called that she needed to sign some papers. To Eileen's alarm, it was papers to donate organs. She called her husband to have the neighbor next door to keep their infant baby son and for her husband to come to the hospital. Joe made it to the hospital as they were taking Brigid to surgery. Brigid stopped breathing. The doctor immediately performed a tracheotomy with a Bic pen in the elevator. Later they performed a permanent trach and took her to intensive care. Then the doctor questioned if there were any siblings at home. "Yes," Eileen said. "We have a newborn." The doctor shook his head. "Hopefully, he won't contract this disease. With a tiny throat, I do not believe we could save that child." A new mother's emotions are already elevated. This sent alarm throughout her body. They kept Brigid in intensive care for two more weeks. At home, Eileen and Joe watched their newborn with fear and trepidation. They truly experienced the fear of not having control when your children need you, but you can't do anything on your own. At this time, Eileen bonded with Father Fagan, who announced to the parish that food would be welcome, and prayers were requested. Both prayers and food were delivered in abundance. That was when Eileen learned you can't be a mother without prayers and community.

Brenda remembers being a new mother with her second child, Justin. She says: I was a fertility patient, so achieving a pregnancy was very much appreciated. My husband and I considered our children as a gift from God. However, following a c- section, when my oldest son Derek was 22 months, circling my knees and pulling at my gown while I held my newborn, I looked to my mother. I asked her--how did a person balance two children at the same time? I felt overwhelmed with both fear and anxiety of two little ones plucking and pulling at me to demand my attention.

Mother said, "Remember how you pray each day for God to help you? Well, . . . Now you pray, but it is **moment by moment.**"

And sure enough, God delivered another blessing 17 months later with the birth of our third son, Vance. That meant three children three years old and younger were now my sons. I still have moment to moment prayers. Control isn't in my hands.

Sometimes an irrational fear is that we think we must **accomplish something big instead of joy in the small things**. We expect our children to be not only the best they can be, but also much better, of course, than we were. Seemingly, we think the next generation will be even better than we were, just because we have gotten wiser with age and experience. David and Brenda believed that their sons took the best characteristics and looks from both to accomplish a "new and improved version." This can bring a high bar of expectations for us and our children. There is joy in relaxing and laughing at the small antics children attack life with. Their sense of humor can improve our sense of humor. There is a saying, "A person without a sense of humor is like a car without springs. You get jolted by every pebble." We can either get constantly jolted or we can relax the tension.

As a grandmother now, Eileen and Brenda can look back at some of our fears and realize that in the big picture, the fears were not such big deals. Some of the mountains look like small hills from this vantage point. Brenda was always trying to create moments for the boys' memories. She had a "theme" birthday party, even when the child was one year old and wouldn't remember the Winnie the Pooh stand up birthday cake (baked by Fran, her sister-in-law). Brenda made a big deal of birthdays; they would extend for several days. It was almost the entire week of celebration rather than one day. One time her son Justin told her that he really looked forward to his birthday party. He followed this with a sigh. He said it was really tiring though. It was exhausting for him, trying to make sure that everyone had a good time at his birthday party. Brenda had not realized that large people-filled parties would put pressure on her young son. As parents, we often create something that looks big to us, but is too much for the child. We expect something big instead of the joy in the small things that would make the child happy.

Eileen remembers worrying over whether the goodie bags at the birthday were good enough. She had previously overheard kids discussing other goodie bags from other parties with comments like, "This is for babies. Or I don't color" as if it were the host's fault. She sweated bullets over the goodie bags. It was a mountain that was a mole hill. Have you noticed the joy that a young child has over playing with the empty box that an expensive toy was wrapped in?

If we are fortunate in a different life stage, our grandchildren break into happy smiles when they see us. We have the gift of time, so we can slow down and enjoy the small things without being pressured by a time schedule. Grandchildren love to hear the stories of when their parents were small, and especially stories of when their parents misbehaved. This helps keep the parents in perspective of how they, too, didn't sleep through the night or struggled with a problem.

 Brenda told her granddaughters they could ask or tell her anything. She really wants to know their thinking in order to deepen connection on both parts. Her granddaughter, Mary Craddock, is experiencing a milestone that is typically nerve wracking. She is practicing driving for her beginners driving license. She says her dad has taught her, but he sometimes reverts to "loud" commands (he calls it motivational speaking—isn't that what dads do?) Her mom rides with her, smiling and nodding, but she has noticed her mom gripping the side panel of the car (isn't that what moms do—smile and encourage while hiding some heartfelt doubts). Even her grandmother has ridden with her and Gram is busy looking down the road, warning about turn signals and danger ahead (isn't that what grandmothers do? Try to warn about some of the twists ahead in life?) So far, so good on the life lessons in learning to drive and strong communication.

Finding the right disciplinary style remains a challenge for parents. Eileen believes that her own parents had the "benign neglect theory." They didn't set curfews or strict boundaries or made rules because they just believed Eileen and her younger brother would "do the right thing." They were very trusting and set a high bar for expectations. This made Eileen feel if she did not have rules or boundaries set, then she was fair game to go the wrong route. Consequently, she would make up her own curfews, so she felt safer. Her mother often remained vague. Her mom threatened that if Eileen didn't "straighten up" she would have to take drastic measures. Since she never illustrated what drastic measures were, Eileen didn't have a clue as to what drastic measures meant. She lived with ambiguity.

This contrasted with Eileen's husband's childhood. Being the only child, her husband Joe never took a free breath. He had very strict parents who had strong clamps to force him into super stardom. Discipline was the path to success and what they said did not allow collaboration. They decided he should be a doctor. He had no interest, inclination, or aptitude for becoming a doctor. He gave it the college try, but it didn't work. Therefore, when Joe and Eileen married, they agreed to take a middle route with reasonable boundaries for their children to follow.

Brenda had a mother who made firm boundaries. In her family there were regular enforced nap times and the expected behavior of "acting like a lady", placing hands behind her back so she didn't touch anything in a visited home and "pretty is as pretty does." Unfortunately, this sometime backfired. While her mother was introducing herself to a new neighbor, Brenda spotted some tulips that would be a perfect welcome gift. With the zest of hospitality, good manners as well as a big imagination, Brenda quickly yanked up a handful of tulips. (Due to the grasp of a small child, these became irregular and droopy stems unfit for a vase.) Brenda smiled broadly as she presented this spindly bouquet to the new neighbor. The neighbor gazed in horror at the one-time-only blooming tulips that this same new neighbor had just planted. The neighbor's reception of the bouquet was decidedly cool. It was back to the "don't touch" despite good intentions rule.

Then, there is the **fear of not spending quality time with our children**. As Shauna Niequist points out in "Present over Perfect", "I know that I needed to work less… the internal voice that tells me to hustle can find a to-do list in my living room as easily as it can in an office. It's not about paid employment . . .if I push enough, I will feel whole. I will feel proud, I will feel happy. What I feel, though, is exhausted and resentful, but with well-organized closets." Guilt can nag whether one is employed or a stay-at-home mom or dad.

On the other hand, research has shown that continually hovering parents (with too much quality time) can limit the imagination and creativity of a child by offering quick solutions in the child's play-time problem solving. A research study showed that children who were rewarded with statements like "good job" when minimal effort was made, did not put as much focused effort as children who were allowed to think, struggle a little and process through a problem-solving attempt.

Further in our pursuit of quality time, Brenda learned the problem of overscheduling a child with too much activity when Justin was in first grade. He came home to announce that he had won the first-grade spelling bee. He would be representing his school in the next round. Brenda was surprised and immediately offered to sit with him to practice for this big event. She opened the pamphlet and started firing words at him in practice sessions thinking she was helping to prepare him. After a few sessions, Justin asked in a small voice if he could do it himself. Studying by himself, at his own comfortable yet motivated pace, was much more beneficial for him. He felt too much pressure from his well-meaning mom. It taught Brenda that at six years old, he was a motivated and competent kid who would achieve, but at his own level and pace. There was a boundary that could be overstepped if she put too much pressure on him. She personally could be comfortable with pressure, but he could not.

She also learned another lesson about "down" time and overscheduling. Having three sons meant that Brenda tried to schedule "fun" events and lots of physical activities including organized sports. In a nightly prayer time as she tucked her sons in bed, she enthusiastically asked her sons, "Didn't we have a fun Saturday? We went to your soccer game, then an afternoon college basketball game and a movie tonight!" A child's sweet voice answered, "Yes, but I didn't get to just play." She thought about that for the next few minutes. She had been going at an adult pace. They craved "down" time. She resolved to slow down on scheduling and cramming too much in her sons' little lives. Just opening the back door and letting the three boys roar into the back yard was stress relief for them (and for Brenda). There was a lot of motion in their commotion. But they needed to simplify.

Now that they are grown, Derek sent an email saying Brenda had taught him a few things. One lesson was Logic: "Only brush the teeth you want to keep." Or More Logic: "If you are going to kill each other, do it outside. I just finished cleaning the den." Of the Weather: "Your room looks like a tornado went through it." Or Religion: "You had better pray that will come out of the carpet." Or Justice: "One day you'll have kids and I hope they turn out just like you." A footnote is that he didn't. Skylar, his daughter, and Brenda's eldest grandchild turned out perfect.

Sometimes our fears of not being a perfect parent are reinforced by very observant children. Eileen says: My son, Brett, was an amazing kid. From an early age, he seemed to be an old man in a pre-school body.

Once, he told me I wasn't listening to him as he told me a long story. I huffed that I certainly was listening, as I folded the laundry. "No", he responded, "you're not listening with your eyes."

Another time, he looked at me critically for quite a while. Finally, he said, "You're not normal." Really?!

I asked what "normal" looked like and he said that it was like a neighbor in our building who wore rollers in her hair and did massive amounts of home cooking. I asked if he wanted me to

BE normal. He answered, "No. Normal is kind of boring. It's vanilla. You're more like a pistachio chocolate chip. That's my favorite flavor." You gotta love that kid.

My all- time favorite "Brett" story was when we were waiting for quarters in Frankfurt. Every day we'd walk our daughter, Brigid, to kindergarten. Brett and I would practice numbers and colors in German as we'd go to the nearby playground. Brett was 3. So were most of the other children – all preschoolers. One day, he came to me in tears. I asked what was wrong. Had he hurt himself? His answer was, "No. But these German kids are smarter than me." When I asked why he explained, "They already speak German."

There is another fear that faces parents and that is the **fear for their children's safety at school**. Unfortunately, it is not new but a continually recurring consequence.

It is little known now, but one of the first outbreaks of violence to a school campus came to the University of Texas on August 1, 1966. Brenda was there. She had been selected as a campus leader for the incoming Freshmen Orientation. Part of the thrill of freshman orientation was a campus tour to familiarize the newbies with the campus.

Brenda remembers: It was 11:35 A.M, hot and muggy in Austin. We could go to the top of the U.T. tower for a finishing touch to the tour or they could be first in line for lunch. It wasn't a hard decision. A quick vote had us jog back to air conditioning and food. Unknowingly, this was a smart move. It turns out we probably would not be alive if we had toured the tower balcony.

At that same time, Charles Whitman, an ex-Marine and engineering student, was already there, setting up his vista as a sniper. He had three rifles, two handguns and a sawed-off shotgun. Just minutes later, at 11:48 A.M, he began firing his

59

rifle on random victims for a five-block radius after he had shot some last-minute visitors to the tower.

When it was reported on the radio, we could see puffs of smoke from the tower and hear the crack of his rifle fire. Fortunately, our dorm building view did not include the sight of the carnage of students and professors hiding among trees or behind flag poles in the flagpole square, pinned by gunfire. Ambulance drivers, police and pedestrians were targets. Whitman wounded 43, killing 13, in a 96-minute gun spree. He had no intent to stop.

It was the first mass murder at a school that has unfortunately been repeated multiple times in the U.S. The result of that massacre spurred the creation of SWAT teams across the United States. Unfortunately, this fear of school safety has had growing repercussions in the U.S. with no resolution.

But also, as parents we have learned that being in harm's way can occur in the home in a matter of moments. Safety can change as soon as you turn your back. Eileen remembers: When we rented a home in Newport News, Virginia, my son Brett was too young for school and day care was slim in the area. He'd stay at home and "help" me. Even though we were renting, I had to question, "Can I live in a bedroom that is painted bordello pink?" The answer was "no." So we contacted the owner for permission to paint it a neutral color. An enthusiastic "yes" was the answer. (I think they hated it, too, but didn't have the time, energy, or money to make the change.)

Happily, I got out one of Joe's old flight suits for cover and laid out the paint for the project. In the time it took for me to climb into the flight suit, Brett had started to "help." He had picked up the paint can and put it—only God knows how—over his head. I heard muffled sounds and found him walking down the hall, covered in paint with a can firmly in place on his little head.

Mothers know that you leap into action in a case like this. First, I pulled the can off his head. Then I picked him up and ran to the bathroom, turning on the shower as I cautioned him to keep his eyes closed. We both climbed into the shower, with me using a face cloth to wipe away the first of many layers of paint from his face. Eyes, nose, ears—all were full of paint. Eventually, I stripped off his clothing and started working on his body. We were both shriveled before I was sure he was ok. I had been talking to God the whole time— and talking to Brett trying to keep him calm. Then, when I was sure we didn't need 911, I called Joe at work and told him to go immediately to the local grocery store and rent a rug shampooer.

It's amazing how much paint can soak into a shag rug in such a short time. We worked for hours. I think the carpet had started to change color in the end. But it was clean—really clean. And the room got painted—without Brett's help.

So, what was the lesson I learned? First, always expect the unexpected—especially when you turn your back on a "helping" preschooler. Second, never buy shag carpeting. Last and probably most important, learn to live with what you have—especially in a rental!

Sometimes, our **fears for a child's safety** can result in overcompensation. Brenda tells the tale of the first ski trip with her family.

Dreaming of a white Christmas, David and I made plans for our three sons' first ski trip. Derek, my oldest son at 10, expected to throw snowballs and zip down the mountain in a king-of-the-hill mode. Justin, my second son at 8 years,

61

expected a cross between ice skating and roller skating. He had become expert at both from attending birthday parties. Vance, with all the confidence of a 7-year-old and baby of the family, expected to race to keep up with his brothers. . . at all costs.

Rumors of no snow and closed upper lifts left us undaunted. It was 55 degrees, brilliant blue December skies with puffs of clouds in Texas. We were on our way to experience snowflakes!

The 10-hour drive to our first stop progressed well. We munched on the sandwiches that Nanny had packed. In the spirit of Christmas, she had colored the bread green and red. Her Christmas obsession hadn't stopped there. This was a woman who had also allowed professional groomers to dye her two pet poodles red and green. Christmas was a big deal to this enthusiastic grandmother. We continued rolling on, stuffed with Nanny's Christmas sandwiches.

 Upon arrival we instructed the boys to pull on waffled long handle underwear, two pairs of socks, a t-neck shirt and finally a snow bib. Neckerchief, snow hat, gloves and warm jacket completed the look, but also protected against the snow. Wearing snow boots, we clattered along with poles and skis. This is added to the waddle. We complimented ourselves on the purchase of tire chains which we certainly did not need, because even a patch of snow had not yet appeared.

After 25 minutes, we finally saw man-made snow. The snow was not on mountain tops, nor on the parking lot, but it <u>was</u> on the lower lift areas. We also noticed a growing line of people milling around the ski school area.

 I had bundled the boys to protect them from the cold snow. It was *still* 55 degrees. At that moment, Justin toppled over in the snow. He fell to the ground complaining of the heat, so I quickly pulled off his coat. He was crying, clutching his stomach and became limp. I got his head between his knees and the ski instructor called her supervisor. He turned Justin upside down like a newborn babe dangling from his fingers, pronouncing altitude sickness with a need to get blood flow to his head. After 2-3 minutes of being upside down, Justin said he felt better, but when he stood up, he became limp like rubber again. The supervisor carried him to the first aid station, where they placed him in a bed, covered him with blankets, applied hot water bottles to his feet and administered oxygen. The rest of my morning was spent watching Justin sleep off his altitude sickness mixed with heat prostration. Unfortunately, I had overdone the ski clothing to keep them warm.

By lunch Justin wobbled to the cafeteria where Derek and Vance boasted the tales of ski school. Full of wedge stops and the bunny slope, they declared themselves ready for bigger challenges. I watched from the parked car while Justin slept and snored in the back seat.

The next morning, he was bright eyed in determination to learn to ski. I started to put on my skis. Vance, after a few turns, decided his stomach was sick. I took my skis off. We waited it out. After an hour, Vance and I proceeded to 30-minute waits in the lift lines. Derek zipped down at what I considered breakneck speed; Vance made his way in snowplow turns without hesitation. Justin announced the zipping and crashing of other skiers was distracting, but I told him it was impossible to make turns standing still. With encouragement, he caught the rhythm and thought that Nastar racing was a real possibility.

I took Vance up the ski lift while David skied down with the other two boys. As we arched high on the ski lift, enjoying the view, Vance's ski fell off his boot and downward from the ski lift. We exchanged fearful glances. He only had one ski. With panic rising, we tried to figure out how to exit a 45-degree angle with only one ski for a wobbly beginner leaning on his mother. Envisioning a tangled mess, together we decided on the solution.

We had come to the same conclusion. We both started yelling "Help." Our wild pointing gestures added to the confusion. We approached what looked like a cliff drop off from our vantage point. Fortunately, the friendly Apache operators just lifted Vance off, above their heads, dropping him with a thud, but upright. An anonymous kind soul brought his lost ski, and we were off. We skied with sunglasses, no jackets, and still brilliant blue skies. The real snowfall, well, it never came. Five satisfied skiers returned to the Apache Motel.

So, what did I learn from my sons? We settled for tans instead of snowflakes. David and I tried to enjoy the zest of three sons yelling "woo hooooo" as they tackled their first ski runs down the mountain. It just wasn't exactly what we had pictured.

Throughout life, it seems God has tapped us on the shoulder with surprises that were not exactly what we had pictured. Somehow it has always turned out better when I waited on the Lord. . . and He gave me strength.

Before we leave the topic of fears of parenting, there is another side. There are fears of not having a child. Brenda is aware of the heartbreak of **wishing for a child and not having success.** She told it like this: After four years of infertility, a gynecologist plopped down on a hospital bedside chair and faced my husband and me. "The surgery was a success, but you probably have a 20% chance of getting pregnant." We were stunned. Our years had been emotionally and physically exhausting, filled with doctor and hospital visits, uncomfortable tests and tear-filled days. Celebrating the news of friends' pregnancies was bittersweet to share in their joy. Everywhere I turned, it seemed there was someone's child to remind me something was missing in my own empty arms. We even borrowed my good friend Kay's young toddler (Eric) to play with. David and I loved it when people said Eric looked just like us.

We had taken it for granted that we would have children when I had these fertility procedures. Now the doctor was saying a measly 20% chance. Just after this announcement by the doctor, a male friend walked in the hospital room. "Well," said our male friend, "when the weatherman says there is a 20% chance of rain, it always rains!" His statement warmed our heart.

Later, my husband and I came to realize that this waiting period was a God wink. It felt like wilderness. God made a baby boy available to us for adoption through an attorney friend. The baby boy was just what we had been praying for. We understood this was not an accident, but God at work-- we were supposed to adopt Derek and become his mommy and daddy. He was the son we had hoped for—a beautiful baby. Derek didn't grow under my heart, but into it. We came to realize that God had a plan for us to be Derek's parents. In God's good time, twenty-two months later, Justin was born to us and seventeen months later, Vance was born without fertility help. Three sons who were three years old or younger now graced our home.

There was motion in that commotion! Mark 8:33 says, "*You do not have in mind the things of God but the things of man.*" We were guilty! We had been trying the rational route and limiting our trust in God's timing.

I feel that my friend Katie described it well. I received a newsletter from Katie and Eric Dotson, missionaries in Ghana. She began her letter with Psalm 139.

You made all the delicate, inner parts of my body and knit me together in my mother's womb. Thank You for making me so wonderfully complex! Your workmanship is marvelous-how well I know it! Psalm 139:13-14

Katie says: When we first got to Ghana the Lord gave Eric and I advice from a dear friend, "Learn to suffer well." We did not know what this would mean to us personally, but HE is teaching us how to work out difficult circumstances, only with Christ, learning to suffer well. Though we often fall short and miss the mark we are becoming more desperate for HIM, leaning on HIM for everything!

Katie continues: After our last miscarriage I felt like my body was going crazy! I started to experience weird pains that would wake me in the middle of the night, and I just didn't feel right. Our last miscarriage set off an odd autoimmune response...but the Lord is even in this!

It came back that I had H Pylori (a digestive tract bacteria common in countries without good water systems.) Through all the pain, discomfort and fear.... I'm at peace. We are at peace! Jesus is near and is the true "peace giver" and my HEALER!!! This is not about H Pylori or miscarriages. It's about Jesus! I have found myself asking, "Lord what are you up to?" "What are you going to do?" ...... "Lord how can I partner with you in this journey of pain?" "Lord what is Your will in this situation?" Maybe you find yourself asking these or similar questions. Asking the question is the easy part but waiting for the answer is difficult at times. It caused me to read further in Psalm 139, vs 23-24. *"Search me, O God, and know my heart; test me and know my anxious thoughts. Point out anything in me that offends you..."*

Katie's description and request for God to know our hearts, our anxious thoughts and to help us mend our ways is the answer for parents or parents-to-be, who need His help. Let's conclude this chapter on parental fears with some specific help!

As parents, we are going to have fears due to overactive imaginations and old personal issues. The best hope for parenting is Colossians 3: 12-17. This is the scripture we began this chapter with: *"clothe yourselves with compassion, kindness, humility, meekness and patience. Bear with one another and, if anyone has a complaint against another, forgive each other, just as the Lord has forgiven you, so you must also forgive. Above all, clothe yourselves with love, which binds everything together in perfect harmony. And let the peace of Christ rule in your hearts, to which indeed you were called in the one body. And be thankful. Let the word of Christ dwell in you richly; teach and admonish one another in all wisdom and with gratitude in your hearts sing psalms, hymns, and spiritual songs to God. And whatever you do, in word or deed, do everything in the name of the Lord Jesus, giving thanks to God the Father through him."*

It feels good when science repeats what we have already learned in the Bible. The Bible tells us to clothe ourselves in kindness. Science has now proven that Kindness is contagious as stated in The Kindness Advantage: cultivating compassionate and connected children by Dale Atkins. If as parents, we do one small act of kindness every day, it promotes changes in our children and ourselves. Scientifically, experiments have shown that there are changes in the brain (endorphins) when we do acts that make us feel good. In turn, the receiver has a flood of good feelings. The receiver then wants to do more because they feel good in this connection. Small joys can have big pay offs.

Eileen and Brenda especially love the picture of dealing with children found in "Currents of the Heart" by Gigi Graham Tchividjian. Gigi nails this! She says: "Children are not so different from kites. They come in various shapes, sizes, and colors. They need someone to help them get started. Some children take a long time to discover the wind, and they struggle again and again to get up. Others seem to catch on quickly and sail through life with ease. . .We hope our sons will soar and our daughters will fly through life with ease and grace. But most of them will get tangled up and need someone to help repair the mess they've made. . .and when they do, they will need loving, patient, tender repair and encouragement before they're able to soar again. . .they need wind—the undergirding and strength that comes from their parents' unconditional love, acceptance, encouragement and prayer."

This is why David in Psalm 72:15 said of his son, *"prayer...shall be made for him continually; and daily shall he be praised."* Don't you love this thought?

What is the wind beneath a child's wings? Prayer and praise. We want our children to soar, but they will get tangled and need that undergirding strength that comes from acceptance. As a parent dealing successfully with our own fears, we truly make a difference in our child's soaring or sinking.

Let's discuss!

1.Clothing yourself with kindness, patience and love as a parent is a daily struggle. Can you give examples?

2. Whether in word or deed, do you combat the struggle of parenthood with thankfulness or gratitude that these little lives have been entrusted to you? In what ways have you shown this to your children?

3, Have you found yourself exhausted and resentful with well-organized closets? Are you present or are you trying to be perfect?

4. Have you found yourself as a parent over structuring your children with "human doing" rather than "human being" activities? What are some examples?

5. Have you achieved a balance in supporting your child without hovering? What are some areas for improvement?

6. What do you think about the description of your child by Gigi Graham Tchividjian as a kite, soaring or sinking? Can you give examples?

Chapter Seven: A Riptide in Singlehood

We have discussed parenthood and fears of marriage. Let us also examine typical fears in singlehood. Being single doesn't mean you are alone. It just means that God is busy writing your love story. Brenda found herself single at 55 years old when she was widowed. She had gone from graduating college to a wedding a week later and marriage for 34 years. Truly, she had never lived alone when her husband died.

Turning to her single women friends, they advised her that it was better to be single, wishing you were married, than to be married wishing you were single. They also cautioned her that being single doesn't mean you are "less than." It means you are smart enough to wait for the one you deserve. Unfortunately, Brenda didn't always follow that advice.

Brenda tells her own story: The three-year journey of David's leukemia was a partnership in that we faced the fight of cancer together. Following his death, the next year was a cocoon of grief and adjustment: not wanting to let go of his memory, riding a roller coaster of wanting to scream but to appear normal, feeling a deep sense of alone-ness that would be followed by a cushion of shock. This deadened the senses. I felt like half a person. I missed the partnership of someone who asked about my day and listened to my answer, who hugged me as I fell asleep and slung a careless arm across me during the night. I missed someone who would help me with decisions, large and small. I didn't want to give in to grief because I didn't want to be a burden or make it harder for my sons, friends, and co-workers. I wasn't trying to be strong; I just didn't want to wallow in self-pity. I never have had the patience for whiners and complainers. (Of course, I noticed that what I called "prayer" might be considered whining and complaining by the Lord).

I decided to hang on to the phrase, "Life isn't about how to survive the storm, but how to dance in the rain." I knew I wanted to dance (but then my small voice said, "It's more fun to dance with a partner.) I began to resent my evening walk, when I noticed that even the ducks swam two by two!
I needed a new direction which took courage. I knew courage was not the lack of fear, but the ability to face it. I had seen courage up close and personal with David's fight against cancer. The last words he had said to me was, "I'm ready." It was time for me to Redesign or Decline.

Often, when you get hurt, it is like a paper cut. The actual injury is much less than the amount of pain at the time. So, I volunteered for a mission trip to Guatemala where 53% of the population goes to bed hungry at night. We worked in Manchen, a girls' orphanage trying to provide homes for girls off the streets who had been abandoned. We wanted the girls to know that they were loved by the Good Shepherd, that the sheep recognized His voice and came to him. As I worshiped with families in a dirt floor church on the side of a volcanic mountain with purple jacaranda trees, I realized that Matthew 6:33 should be my direction: *"Seek first the kingdom of God and his righteousness, and all these things will be added to you."* I needed to stop gathering knowledge from the outside and gather it from the inside where God and his righteousness were in my heart.

Thus began my journey of Singleness.

Do you know what the number one selling candy bar is internationally? It is Snickers. Yes, I am a Snickers fan. Do you know what "hangry" is? It is when you get grumpy and angry because you are hungry. A Snickers candy bar satisfies hangry. You feel great but it is only for a short time. It is only a short-term satisfaction. It means you did not wait for healthy choices. You did not wait for what you deserve, but you settled for less.

It's as simple as Dr. Seuss: *"You have brains in your head. You have feet in your shoes. You can steer yourself in any direction you choose. You're on your own. And you know what you know. You are the guy (gal) who'll decide where to go."*

What am I getting around to saying? I rushed my Singlehood. I knew better. I had heard, "You can never be happy as someone's other half unless you can be happy as a whole all on your own." Or "If you're single, focus on being a better you. A better you will attract a better next."

No, unfortunately, I had a brief Snickers marriage. Short, satisfying a craving, but unhealthy.

Let's just say, I was hangry, running "from" being single rather than running "to" the right partner. It did not help that he had an old girlfriend that he forgot to give up. Unknown to me, there were three of us in this Snickers marriage almost from the first. Fortunately, the other woman telephoned me to let me know about her being involved just before our third anniversary. It was a surprise to me. Once again, I became Single.

The Fear of being Single (FOBS) is associated with settling for less in relationships. It is a perfectly normal fear since humans are genetically oriented to connection and a desire for a partner to provide safety or security. FOBS is that small voice inside you that nudges you to go on a second date even though you aren't feeling it or go to dinner with a co-worker's third cousin "who is perfect for you." Or indulging in online dating where finding a prince among the frogs is humorous. Many women have stated that they don't like to go to a restaurant, movie or wedding for fear of being perceived as defective or "less than" if they don't show up with a partner. FOBS is alive and well even in the most courageous of women.

However, women are discovering an important concept. As author and speaker Marilyn Ferguson once wrote, "Ultimately we know deeply that the **other side of every fear is a freedom**." As Eileen and Brenda earlier stated, taking small steps to build inner confidence and build up your self-worth results in quality relationships. These unhurried steps and not accepting less are worth our time and effort. There is a freedom on the other side of FOBS.

It was back to the drawing board and the Bible.

Would you believe if I said Haggai 1:2-7 gave me an answer? I hardly knew that Haggai was a book in the Bible. Stay with me here. "Thus says the Lord of hosts: *These people say the time has not yet come to rebuild the Lord's house. Then the word of the Lord came by the prophet Haggai, saying: Is it a time for you yourselves to live in your paneled houses, while this house lies in ruins? Now therefore thus says the Lord of hosts: Consider how you have fared. You have sown much and harvested little; you eat, but you never have enough; you drink, but you never have your fill; you clothe yourselves, but no one*

74

is warm; and you that earn wages earn wages to put them into a bag with holes. Thus says the Lord of hosts: Consider how you have fared."

In other words, you are working hard, but there is a leak in the system. You may be chasing the wrong things, with the wrong priorities. Or in the famous words of Dr. Phil, "How is that working for you?"
I mentioned that I had realized the answer earlier, but I had gotten caught in the Riptide of Fear. I had allowed myself to drift further from the shore just like a riptide, getting away from my list of what I wanted in a partner. I lost my priority.

Once again, I had to reread Matthew 6:31-34: *"Therefore do not worry, saying "What will we eat? Or what will we drink? Or what will we wear? For it is the Gentiles who strive for all these things and indeed your heavenly Father knows that you need all these things. But* <u>*seek first for the kingdom of God and his righteousness and all these things will be given to you as well*</u>. *So do not worry about tomorrow, for tomorrow will bring worries of its own. Today's trouble is enough for today."*

I knew what a good marriage was. I got caught in the riptide of fear of Singleness and drifted in my expectations. My friends were all married. I really didn't want to start the games of dating. As an English major in college, I read Shakespeare's Sonnet #116, "Love is not love which alters when alteration finds . . .an ever-fixed mark that looks on tempests and is never shaken. It is the star to every wandering bark. . .Love's not time's fool, though rosy lips and cheeks within his bending sickle come. . .but it bears it out to the edge of doom." I knew when I married David that my marriage would last until we were old and gray, or death separated us.

Now was a different story. At this point, I could relate to Jehoshophat. King Jehoshophat of Judah, cried out, "What do I do, Lord?" The answer to Jehoshophat and me was: Do not be discouraged. Pray to me and I will deliver you. <u>For the</u>

battle is not yours, but mine." Obviously, I had to turn the battle over to the Lord!

Unfortunately, I have always found that His timeline is not as fast as my timeline.

And what about the waiting? That's where Romans 8: 18 comes in. *Waiting does not diminish us. We are enlarged in our expectancy. The longer we wait, the more the Holy Spirit is there to intercede with groans that words can't express. He searches our heart (8:26) and intercedes.*

Yes, I am still single. This is not to say I have not had an interesting journey in my Singlehood. I tried the online thing for a short period.

Let me entertain you with some of my brief but interesting online experiences. One of my first dates immediately hugged me, assured me he was in international banking (later revealed that was an internship many years ago and for the last 12 years had a blue-collar job. His job was not the magnitude he pretended), and that he was immediately going off online dating that very night because I was exactly what he wanted. (I was not assured that was a good thing.) His follow up phone call informed me that he knew I would check the internet and oh, by the way, yes, he had been filed against for sexual harassment. Hmmm.

As he walked to the door on our second date, he assured me that if we married, I wouldn't have to change my name and that he was really smitten. (Talking marriage? On the second meeting?) But the full court press didn't ring true to me, and I think he got the message. I was ghosted. He was back online with new pictures the next day.

The next guy was shorter than his picture but had very blue eyes. I was attracted to his consulting experience which read like my consulting experience. I thought we had this in common. He represented himself as consulting with a major firm, retiring at 55 so he could regain his life. He said his 30-year marriage suffered from his extensive travel. This could have been true, but strangely he didn't recognize some of my consulting terms and was puzzled when we talked business. After a few dates, he concluded that I am family-centric and church-centric. He is neither. I am not sure what centric he was up to, but it had something to do with fishing. Later I was contacted by the online dating service. They said they had received complaints about him, and they couldn't be held responsible if I dated him. Scary.

Another guy scheduled to meet me for a first date on Sunday at 6PM, but then cancelled to say his grandson had broken his ankle in Houston and he was flying there to help. That sounds rational. But I was talking with a friend who mentioned her date for Sun at 6 PM had been cancelled because of an injury to his grandson's ankle. Busted! Same guy booked us both for the same time. Maybe it was an oversight because he had so many women he was juggling around. I never heard from him again.

I got an online scam too. Beware if they say they are an engineer/architect and suddenly get called away to a far country and never seem to meet you in person first. They become pen pals online. They call and say all the right things, but somehow, they can't send a current picture of themselves in their new job in a foreign country. His excuse was that he only had a flip phone. Really? My guy got angry when I said I didn't believe his story, but he couldn't quite locate a phone to take a picture of him in his new job surroundings to prove his point.

These scams are rampant and intelligent women fall for them. After warming into her heart, one friend had money requests of several thousand dollars several times in a year- long telephone romance. Finally, she had the calls traced to Nigeria, but the money was lost. He was not who he said he was. My hairdresser got a request from her online sweetie to cash a company check for $5000. He said he was offshore and couldn't cash the check. He gave step by step instructions on the phone to help her go to her bank and deposit the check in her account. She then wired him the money from her account. The next day the bank called to say it was a phony check. My hairdresser got stuck with having to make the check good.

My singleness has been quite a journey. I have had an interesting path from dating a doctor who wasn't really divorced to a doctor 12 years younger than me who was always calling to date me in between his online flings. Also, even when I was with this doctor, women would fling themselves at him while I was standing there. One woman at a party said," Doctor, heal me" and deposited a big kiss on his lips. He may have pursued this healing, but not while I was standing there. I dated newly widowed and newly divorced men who are in love with ghosts. I dated a handsome, loving, intelligent man who just could not help but fabricate. Blowing smoke was so continual, he fooled himself. He was a big fan of the lies he told himself.

Then there was the date looking for what we call "a nurse or a purse" syndrome. He confessed to a recent heart attack, no car, and living in an apartment because his sister got tired of his bumming from her. He needed a nurse and a purse.

I laugh because my stories are the same as many of my single friends. Or sometimes their stories are much worse. On the other hand, I know that one friend of mine has had success after 60 tries. She says you just must persevere.

So how does this play out in our Singlehood? In Victor Frankel's book "Man's Search for Meaning," he says, "Don't aim for success—the more you aim at success and make it a target, the more you are going to miss it. Success like happiness must ensue, the side effect of dedication to a cause greater than oneself."

Or we can consider what Mordecai said to Esther, "*Who knows, maybe you have come to this position, to fulfill your destiny. Who knows? God knows.*" Esther 4:14.

Again, what is the answer to FOBS? Small steps build self-confidence and getting out of your comfort zone allows new people into your life. Here is my short quick prayer for me and you:

Dear God,

Shatter my superficiality so that I may walk in strength and with dignity to my destiny. Help supply me with this strength and dignity as I discover the why and how of what I'm supposed to accomplish in Your name and for You.
Amen

Let's Discuss

1. Have you been hiding behind excuses and accepting less in your Singlehood? Can you think of some examples?

2. Have you neglected the gift and your destiny that is in you which was given to you by God because you have been searching for Mr. Right in all the wrong places?

3.If God is your co-pilot, do you realize you need to switch places? He needs to be in the pilot's seat.   Instead, when He leads, can you follow? What would that look like in your life?

4. Have you looked for transformation and a new direction in yourself in your Single life? What would transformation look like and what are the first steps you need to take? **Redesign or decline!**

Chapter Eight: **Professional Fears—An Expensive Habit!**

"So don't throw away your confidence—it brings a great reward. You need to endure so that you can receive the promises after you do God's will. In a little while longer, the one who is coming will come and won't delay...Hebrews 10: 35-37

As Erma Bombeck said, "Think of all those women on the Titanic who waived away the dessert cart." Adventure awaits if we don't hold back because of self-induced fears. These fears plague us in our professional life. Our internal self-dialogue often causes us to struggle with insecurities. That inner voice may not whisper "you can do this" but instead cautions us with "don't blow this!"

Serena Williams, ranked #1 tennis player in the world for multiple consecutive years, says: "I play a lot of tennis. So how do I have confidence to make that crucial shot? I stay with it, and I pray a lot of prayers." Great advice!

In other words, we allow the lack of confidence and fear for our capability to distract us in our perfect follow-through. We get derailed. Fear has become so ingrained that it has become an expensive habit. We sometimes have normalized the trauma. One of the best descriptions of the #MeToo movement was an item by Susan Polley in The New York Times.

"Several years ago, I approached a couple of successful female actors in Hollywood about an idea I had for a comedy project: We would write, direct and star in a short film about the craziest, worst experience we'd ever had on a set. We told our stories to one another, thinking they would be hysterically funny. We were full of zeal for this project. But the stories, when we told them, left us in tears and bewildered at how casually we had taken these horror stories and tried to make them into comedy. They were stories of assault. When they were spoken aloud, it was impossible to reframe them any other way. This is how we'd normalized the trauma, tried to integrate it, by making comedy out of it. We abandoned the film, but not the project of unearthing the weight of these stories, which we'd previously hidden from ourselves.

Harvey Weinstein may be the central-casting version of a Hollywood predator, but he was just one festering pustule in a diseased industry. The only thing that shocked most people in the film industry about the Harvey Weinstein story was that suddenly, for some reason, people seemed to care. That knowledge alone allowed a lot of us to breathe for the first time in ages.

Here is an unsettling problem that I am left with now: Like so many, I knew about him. And not just from my comparatively tame meeting with him. For years, I heard the horrible stories that are now chilling so many people to their core. Like so many, I didn't know what to do with all of it. I've grown up in this industry, surrounded by predatory behavior, and the idea of making people care about it seemed as distant an ambition as pulling the sun out of the sky.

I want to believe that the intense wave of disgust at this sort of behavior will lead to real change. I think that many people in high places will be a little more careful. But I hope that when this moment of noisy sisterhood dissipates, it doesn't end with a woman in a courtroom, being made to look crazy, as these stories so often do."

Eileen and Brenda think that the #MeToo movement did bring change in opportunities for women. It brought attention to the fact that women normalized fears.

However, we need to think of the turtle. *He can't make progress until he sticks his neck out.*

Often, it isn't lack of talent or ability that gets in the way of career progress. It is our *mindset*. A Hewlett Packard study found that when a higher-level position would open within the company, men would apply if they felt they had 60% of the skillset required for the job, whereas women would only apply if they felt they had 100% of the skills required! In other words, women let **their fear of not being perfect** run their show.

Cortney Baker, a friend, CEO, Career Consultant/Coach, and podcast producer puts it in her own words in a newsletter:
 After months of working for a home healthcare company that didn't value me, I decided that I could do what they were doing. And I would do it better. I would treat my employees with the respect they deserve and automatically the business would be a huge success.

I may have been a 27-year-old mom with ZERO business experience, but I was determined to make a go of it. Oh, and did I mention that I was also pregnant with baby #2, the ink was barely dry on my brand-new mortgage, and my husband had just lost his job?

I had impeccable timing...

Despite all of that, we filed the incorporation paperwork and waited for the great state of Texas to make my new company official. And that's when the trash talk kicked in.

You know what I'm talking about...that nagging voice that likes to convince you you're not capable of pulling this off and you're crazy to even try.

I call mine Lucy and let's just say Lucy likes to run her mouth. For months, Lucy was giving me the beatdown. I started to doubt myself and I'd question everything. And finally, I just accepted the fact that I had no business starting my own company. I tucked that dream up on a shelf for *someday*...maybe. I thank God that wasn't the end of the story; after months of letting Lucy have her way, everything came to a head.

I'd spent the day driving around Dallas, risking my life in a freak ice storm so I could get to all the therapy clients I had that day when I found out I wouldn't be getting my paycheck. My bosses simply "forgot" to run payroll, which meant the first mortgage payment on the cute little house we just bought wasn't going to clear.

At that moment, I knew I could not do it anymore. I needed to change the thoughts and beliefs Lucy had been planting in my brain and come up with some new ones that would serve me because I HAD to make a better life for my family.

I gave it all up to God that day and told Him that if I was meant to do this, I was going to need a little guidance. That's when things started to shift. Of course, it doesn't mean there were no struggles along the way. I can assure you, there were plenty! But shifting my mindset gave me the confidence to figure things out as I went along so I could keep moving forward-- even when it didn't look pretty.

I can't imagine how different my life would look today if I'd let Lucy (instead of God) determine my fate. I *do* know I wouldn't have built an 8-figure business from the ground up and I wouldn't be writing to you today to let you know that if *I* could do it, *you* can do it!"

Thanks, Cortney! (By the way, Brenda met Cortney on a mission trip to China where they conducted seminars for 300 male and female Chinese, eager to learn how to have success in business). Women, especially, have **a fear of being overwhelmed.** We pass on bigger projects that could boost our career up the ladder because we feel overwhelmed and non-perfect. We let Lucy have her way! Cortney has mentioned shifting her mindset "even when it didn't look pretty." This is expressed beautifully by Dana Belmore, my missionary friend in her June 2019 newsletter from Alaska. Let's tune in to what Dana writes about being overwhelmed with her house project, following the Earthquake 2019 in Alaska:

From November until the end of May, my kitchen decor included blue painters' tape, plywood, and a black utility trash bag. Thanks to the earthquake, a jagged crack blew through the most extensive section of my countertops and across the glass stovetop, leaving behind three semi-functional and moody burners plus a cranky oven. I also had a broken dishwasher, a leaking, stinky sink, a busted refrigerator, and multiple cracks in the walls. These were the problems we could see.

Amazing what hidden gems you discover when you start ripping your kitchen apart.

Good gravy, Chip Gaines, renovations ARE NOT THAT FUN. I vaguely recall several people warning me of the Renovation Blues, but I was probably too preoccupied with demolition and flooring samples and overwhelmed by dreams of a kitchen without a fault line to pay much mind. Sheesh. Even my dog is down and sick, suffering from allergy-induced bronchitis.

And to add further insult to my supposed southern toughness, you'd think a South Louisiana-raised girl would have a hard time succumbing to complaints over the record-breaking Alaskan summer heat. But according to my thermometer, it's 89 degrees outside and 80 degrees inside my house. (Some places in Anchorage broke 100.) Remember, this is Alaska. NO in-home air conditioning. Super long, hot days of intense rays. (There's a scientific reason it feels hotter here at 75 degrees than back home. Promise. Google it.). Some people have taken to pitching tents in their yards or sleeping in their RVs. To make things even more interesting, we've been suffering from cottonwood-induced allergy attacks, smoke from the now 90k-plus burning Peninsula-area acreage, threats of more wildfires, and enough Sheetrock dust to finger-write this newsletter.

All this fun stuff has left me one big coughing, itchy, sweaty mess who's surviving on Zyrtec, Special K cereal, Instant Pot boiled eggs, Tillamook Mudslide Ice Cream, and coffee. I've got a sneaky suspicion that renovations are a lot like childbirth, and I'm already psyched about dis-remembering this pain.

But onto the GOOD STUFF. Because amid this haze, heat and hard, God is moving.

God places us in areas where we might be uncomfortable or where we might not want to be in, but He has a purpose for why we are appointed there. It's our own willingness to surrender and obey that shows us the amount of trust we have in him.

A 7.2 earthquake rocked our world and exposed all things needing immediate attention.

And THAT is what He wants me to see right now.

I look around my upside down and ripped out home and *yes*, I spy subfloor and wiring, but I also see the work of my Refiner. Goodness, this demo and reno isn't just for the house. It's for *me!* And the biggest lesson of all being *because He loves*. So yes, the process of growing up and deep—this daily intentionally choosing to please Jesus over pleasing my mortal flesh—brings pain. Pruning. Exposure. Ugh. Too many times I'm caught up in what I want or need or fear or expect that I close myself off to what God has for me.

He sure is good at placing us in areas that create discomfort and frustration and leaves us wanting to hide in the bathroom, clinging fast to our don't-wants and can't-dos, isn't He? But He's so, so GOOD. His appointments and plans, pruning and refining and growing are *for* us. All for His glory and our good because He *loves*. The question is, do we trust Him enough to lay down our fears, expectations, and demands? Better yet, do I *welcome* His refining fire? If *you know what God has for you, the first step is to just say yes.*"

Therefore, as Cortney and Dana have pointed out, we have fears that we don't trust the Lord with. Often, we have a **fear of leaving our job,** so we try to take on two jobs. We keep our day job and try the dream job that matches our passion as a part time effort.

87

Cortney Baker calls this a side hustle. Since she is a professional consultant, she gives advice to her mentees in the following newsletter:

When you're still in the side hustle phase of your business, it's your dream of taking it full time that propels you through the daily grind of managing life with two careers.

I know the struggle of trying to do it ALL when you're getting your business off the ground. It can be pretty tempting to jump ship from your 9-5 sooner rather than later but there are **4 things you'll need to have on lock down to take your own biz full time** and give it the best chance of success.

How To Manage Your Time - If there's one thing I know for sure, time is your biggest asset--in business and in life. Your time is valuable; you can't make more of it, so you want to be dang sure you're very intentional about how you're using it!

I know I personally do not use my time wisely when things aren't scheduled, so you'd better believe EVERYTHING goes on my calendar. I also set my phone on airplane mode and block out specific days for certain tasks to avoid wasting time scrolling social media and reading emails when I've got work to do.

How To Manage Your Money - When you're just starting out in your business, money is tight, so there won't be a lot of it to manage. That's why it's super important to have a budget and pay close attention to every dollar coming in and going out. And, unless those $10 venti non-fat caramel Frappuccino double espresso lattes come with a shot of gold, sister, they aren't worth it!

But I know it can be really tempting to spend money on all the things you could possibly need for your biz, but you want to be sure it's 100% necessary for the growth of your company before laying out the cash (or slapping down your credit card) for it. Some other things to think about would include where you might be able to cut expenses and what tools would be helpful for managing your books.

Your Action Plan - I have no doubt you've got big dreams...as a budding entrepreneur, it's in your DNA! But you don't want to leave the success of your biz to chance...you need a plan of action, broken down step-by-step, so you know just what to do and when you're going to do it.

What's also critical is finding a tribe of like-minded women to support you and hold you accountable to your goals. Sometimes the encouragement of another person going through exactly what you're going through is enough to keep you moving in the right direction. Sometimes all it takes is that extra push off the ledge to help you see you really can fly!

Your priorities - There will be lots of shiny objects to distract you along the way to becoming your own CEO. Be prepared for the self-doubt and trash talk to kick in right about the time you think you might be ready to hand in your resignation. Keep the focus on your priorities. And when you're tempted to divert your attention in another direction, ask yourself if what you're considering will ultimately get you to the finish line...or is it just interrupting the race?

If your goal is to become your own boss, you can have the biggest dreams and an airtight business plan but if you don't have the mindset and the tools you need to make it happen, the journey will feel a lot like you're running an uphill marathon backward in HEELS. "

Frazzled, frustrated and fragmented. Even J.K. Rowling considered two jobs. J.K., whose Harry Potter books have sold more than 400 million copies was told by her editor that she needed to get a day job because she would never be able to make a living writing a children's book. In her 2008 Harvard address, she admitted "What I feared most for myself at your age **was not poverty, but failure**." Her first manuscript was rejected by multiple publishing houses. She said, "It is impossible to live without failing at something, unless you live so cautiously that you might as well not have lived at all—in which case, you fail by default."

Sometimes, however, there is a **fear of success.** In other words, you may get what you ask for. A friend continually made the case for working from home to her boss and after a year, she was allowed to work from her home. After a few months, she realized that she missed going into the office as it was a very real part of her social life. She missed lunches. She missed the social interaction that let her network. She began to feel isolated and that she had decreased visibility for her career. Yes, she had less traffic or commute, but she wasn't convinced that the trade-off was working in her favor. Another friend wanted a better paying position, but she would have to give up some personal freedom and family time, while gaining more travel time and more responsibility. When she weighed her options, she knew this would lead to a great deal more stress and the negatives outweighed the positives.

This brings up another stressor and fear that our career **is taking away quality time from our family.**

 Michele Obama recounted in her book, Becoming, a lesson that she learned after her first baby arrived: "and this would also go into my file of things many of us learn too late—is that a part-time job, especially when it's meant to be a scaled-down version of your previously full time job, can be something of a trap. . . At work, I was still attending all the meetings I always had while also grappling with most of the same responsibilities. The only real difference was that I now made half my original salary and was trying to cram everything into a twenty-hour week. If a meeting ran late, I'd end up tearing home at breakneck speed to fetch Malia so we could arrive on time (Malia eager and happy, me sweaty and hyperventilating) to the afternoon Wiggleworms class at a music studio on the North Side of Chicago.

To me it felt like a sanity-warping double bind. I battled guilt when I had to take work calls home. I battled a different sort of guilt when I sat at my office distracted by the idea that Malia might be allergic to peanuts. Part time work was meant to give me more freedom, but mostly it left me feeling as if I were only half doing everything, that all the lines in my life had been blurred."

She felt she was working twice as hard for half the pay.

Consequently, an important question to ask yourself is: "What am I really asking for and why?". Investigate the opportunities by paying attention to your own voice. Know what gives you peace and fulfillment and seek the advice of role models.

Brenda has taken some chances in her professional life. In her mid-twenties, she gave up teaching to work directly in Couture (plus Human Resources) at Neiman Marcus in Houston. Fashion had always been a passion for her. She took the opportunity to work directly with Lawrence Marcus. She learned fashion and marketing strategy from this legend in the fashion world. This led to becoming a co-CEO when she created a children's resale shop with her friend and neighbor, Ann Taibo. The resale of fine children's clothes was a novelty at the time. The shop received immediate television exposure and their shop "Clothes for Kids" did very well.

The shop was interrupted by a move to Ft Worth which gave her the chance to be an Adjunct Professor at Texas Christian University. That led to a desire to gain a Ph.D. At 40, she started working for General Dynamics while attending The University of Texas at Austin (a 3-hour commute) to both work full time and attend the University Ph.D. program. Due to her doctorate, she next worked as a management consultant in her 40's and 50's. In her 60's she watched HGTV and believed that she, too, could flip houses. She left consulting after 20 years to renovate upper end houses. Due to excellent work crews (thank you, Juan and Pete), good realtors (thank you Sandy and Courtney Petruska), her management and business skills helped satisfy her passion for interior design. She has now "flipped" fourteen houses. She is looking forward to her next adventure.

Eileen started her career with the nerves and anxiety that student teaching can bring:

There were no Student Teaching positions in Queens for St. John's University Seniors in 1967. There had been a strike at St. John's a few years earlier and the cries of "Academic Freedom" still echoed in many school administrators' memories. They closed the doors to aspiring teachers from St. John's. I found a placement in Westbury, in "distant" Nassau County. The good news was that it was a high school minutes away from my Grandparents' house, so lunch was free and delicious.

I was nervous, as you would expect. I would be working as an intern for the Chairman of the English Department. There was a lot riding on doing well. He explained that one of his classes came from a nearby Correctional Facility. Those students were fairly remedial, and some had "special" problems. "John" would have visions of his dead Grandmother, rising through the cracks in the linoleum. He advised it was wise never to step on a crack. "Armondo" was known to carry a knife in his boot, so staying away from that leg was advisable. Oh, and Antonio Possilipo was coming, straight from Italy. He had no English skills. Other than that, the chairman stated there was nothing special.

To reassure me about teaching Antonio, he tossed a booklet onto the desk and said it would help. It was "The Soldiers Guide to Italy," World War II wisdom in communicating with the locals with such useful phrases as "When do the trains come through?", "Tanks!" and "Do you like chocolate?" I was less than impressed. Thankfully, another student was a recent arrival to the States from Italy, and he spoke English well. We made a trio – speak to one, translate to the other and repeat. It was a beginning. Those were the days that I learned to improvise, and it influenced my career. I became a specialist in English as A Second Language, a field in which I spent most of my teaching career.

I learned more than the students that year. And I survived. I was afraid, but I gained confidence as well as experience. It would have been very easy to turn tail and head for the door that first day. Staying on took determination – and prayer.

I retired after 40 years in the classroom. My husband says I taught "cradle to the grave" - from an international pre-school in Germany to Cambodian "Boat People" who were illiterate in their own language, some in their 70s and 80s. I loved it. And who knows what I would have done instead if I hadn't placed my fears in God's hands and stepped through the door to my future?

Remember, as the angels told Abraham he would have a son, his elderly wife Sarah laughed. It didn't seem possible or probable. When God called Moses to lead His people, Moses made excuses. The world is impressed with kings. The Bible is impressed with servants. God can bring good, even though we fail. He doesn't pick the most capable, but the most trusting who have an expensive habit of fear, yet they stick with it and pray! A local pastor has said, "He doesn't call the qualified, he qualifies the called!"

This brings up the final **fear of not being good enough.** Dana Belmore, the friend and missionary quoted earlier, talked about a tour in England called The Christian Heritage Tour: "We took a walk. But not through the touristy hot spots. Instead, we walked in the footsteps of Martin Luther, John Wesley, and more. But here's the rub. I tend to heed the quiet whisper that taunts me with the lie, "These men were used because they were great people, Dana. Who are you?" Our guide reminded me of the truth. These people didn't set out to change the world. They were ordinary people keenly aware of their sinful, fallen nature, but their love for Jesus had them embracing repentance, obedience, and sacrifice even when flesh and fear overwhelmed them. They cherished Christ above security. Wealth. Fame. Power. Freedom. Comfort. These great men of faith rose every morning with the same choice I rise to—follow Christ or follow me. And despite pushbacks and threats and persecution, they chose Jesus over self. Like dominoes, one man's obedience impacted another man's life, and another and another and the world has never been the same. And why do I sometimes believe big, bold leaps of faith and public displays of good deeds and generosity for sure outrank personal, significant steps of faith and simple, unpublished acts of service? These men didn't seek fanfare and notoriety; they just loved Him and served well."

We must check our **fear of not being good enough**. Is there a bully chipping away your confidence at your workplace? Eileen says, I, too, have doubted myself after I turned fifty. Only once have I questioned my direction in terms of a career. Since childhood, I have always wanted to be a teacher. There was no question that I pursue it as a career. I came to see it as who I was. Then, I questioned myself.

I had been working in a local community college. The director of the program was a difficult person. I've been told that I could make friends with a rock. Not with this woman. She began to make changes in my syllabus, question my lesson plans, "visit" my classroom, and make strong suggestions about changing my approach to ESL. I began to seriously doubt myself. All this doubt and drain crowded in on me after how many years of teaching? This became a wilderness of unexpected pain and constant badgering on doing something I loved. Finally, the tension led me to the decision to quit at the end of the semester.

When I left, I didn't know what I was going to do. Had I fooled myself about my life's work? Should I find a new direction? Then, the phone rang.

I thought the person was a fellow reporter from my son's newspaper. He asked many questions about ESL. I thought it was for an article for the paper. Then, he asked me to go to his office. I was thinking, "Pushy reporter". When I asked why, he said he thought I knew – he was offering me a job as Director of the ESL Program for my region. I stayed, quite happily, at that job until I retired, some 12 years later. Thank you, God.

Some years later, I asked this lovely man where he had gotten my name in the first place. He said he'd hoped I would never ask. He found it in his desk with a note "Good ESL teacher – call her". Yes, thank you, God! You answered a prayer before I knew to pray.

Do we look in the mirror and believe the old Saturday Night routine, which is. . ." we're good enough, we're smart enough and . . . People like me!" Do we **Redesign or decline**?

It is comfortable to stay just where we are. In John 5, we learn of a man who had been on a mat for 38 years. Several disabled people would lie by the Bethesda pool believing the pool healed people when it rippled. When Jesus passed by the disabled man, he stopped to ask the invalid, "Do you want to get well?" The invalid answered with an excuse (I have no one to help me into the pool when the water is stirred.) Then Jesus said to him, "Get up! Pick up your mat and walk." Jesus didn't say," I will make you comfortable. Go get a pillow."

Jesus gave the invalid man three steps.

1) He asks him if he wants to do something he has not done in his entire life. (Get well)
2) He eliminates a relapse into old ways and lifestyle (Pick up your mat)
3) He expects continued success by taking action (Walk!)

Can you do this? Will you Redesign or decline? Faith is a deliberate personal choice. As we choose to trust God daily, our faith grows. Is there something we need to ask God to do for us that we have been making excuses about?

Let's examine this perseverance. Linda Hollander who started The Bag Ladies, a manufacturer of custom bags for shopping malls, etc. said that it was hard for her to imagine owning her own business. However, in her book ***Bags to Riches: Success Secrets for Women in Business***, she writes that "fear is the most expensive habit you will ever have."

She offers a technique to overcome fear called sensory anchoring. This means you force your inner voice to support you, rather than allowing that inner voice to tear down your efforts. Remember the three steps that Jesus used for the invalid? It is the same step by step.

Here's how sensory anchoring works.
1) Recall in vivid detail a positive confidence experience from your past. It could be a time when you conquered a tough assignment or a time when others were extremely proud and complimented you. Picture firmly in your mind that ultimate rush of confidence and euphoria. (Jesus asked—do you want to get well?)

2) When you begin to feel fearful, think about one of these positive experiences instead of making an excuse. This memory supports your confidence and courage. (Jesus said, "Pick up your mat.")

3) This cannot make your problems go away but helps you take the next step forward. (Walk!)

Professional athletes do this same imaging. In the Olympics before making that dive, skate, or gymnastic move, they picture an image of a perfect success. They review exactly what it looks and feels like to make the perfect move. Their brain and muscles follow through by executing that same motion. Practice means that they do not let doubt interfere with that motion.

As we choose to trust God daily, our faith grows. He knows our heart. He knows our actions. He gives us the power to change thought patterns. *We do not need to pray for tasks equal to our power. We need to pray for power equal to our tasks.*

Professionally, how do we face those fears? Is there something we need to act on, knowing that God will give us the strength to do the impossible? Remember the earlier quote from Serena Williams. "How do I make those crucial shots? I stay with it, and I pray a lot of prayers!"

Let's Discuss

1. Do you fear failure? When the voice in your head said you should give up, what did you do? Did you take the risk or turn back?

2. In Luke's Gospel, Jesus spoke of "counting the cost." Prayerfully, do you ask "what are the good and bad outcomes of this decision?

3.Author Nora Roberts said, "If you don't go after what you want, you'll never have it. If you don't ask, the answer is always no. If you don't step forward, you are always in the same place." Have you found yourself in the same place? What does this quote mean to you?

Chapter Nine: Health Fears

The last fear we will discuss is fears over our health. This fear
is universal—we don't worry until strange symptoms emerge.
Then this fear is often riddled with irrational behavior. The
coronavirus heightened awareness of illness as never before.
Then, internet technology gave us multiple sources to self-
diagnose our symptoms.

Our health fears can fall into two categories: **nosophobia and
hypochondria. Nosophobia** is when a person becomes afraid
of a specific disease and is constantly looking for these
symptoms to start. Medical students, due to exposure to people
with diseases, or Grey's Anatomy television addicts (and that
includes many of us) can develop an irrational fear that they
have the symptoms of some exotic diseases. With the onset of
the coronavirus, we became a nation of nosophobics.

Previously, to sneeze in public was followed by "God bless you." With the onset of the pandemic, to sneeze in public was to evacuate a Starbucks with social distancing or a stampede. Previously, in times of crisis or trouble, the churches would be filled with people looking for comfort. With the pandemic, churches were asked to be empty. Fortunately, God is an expert at dealing with uncertain times.

On the other hand, **hypochondria** is becoming easily alarmed when an actual symptom does occur. Hypochondria is a recognized psychiatric disorder which affects an estimated 1 to 5 percent of Americans. It exists in a continuum, from people who simply worry excessively about their health to those who are completely debilitated by fear. True hypochondriacs don't make up fake symptoms and imaginary pains to get attention. Instead, when a genuine symptom appears, they extend this thought to magnified proportion.

For those who have hypochondria, instead of feeling relieved when they get a positive diagnosis, they will brood. They think about the cancer in hiding, or the disease they "just know" the doctor didn't catch. This may progress to a consuming brooding that interferes with work, or future happy events. Stress can lead to more symptoms. For people debilitated by hypochondria, antidepressants and therapy may help. But, often, hypochondriacs do not realize that they are one. So, what are the signs of hypochondria? The signs are irrational fear: becoming easily alarmed over a symptom, and constant talking, thinking and re-thinking about health issues with this symptom in particular. All of us have a bit of hypochondria. Reframing our irrational thoughts is difficult.

In this 21st century, quarantines or self-isolation from the coronavirus was a new development. Confinement could last from fourteen days minimum to an extended period. Eileen experienced going from being healthy to confinement in one quick moment. This was not due to the coronavirus but from a freak accident the year before. She describes it with lessons learned.

From Eileen: Being confined ratchets up emotion and wears down the disposition. It's safe to say that most of us have known an older relative who complains. They dislike giving up their cars, not shopping for their own groceries, making frequent trips to doctors, not being able – physically- to get up and go… wherever and whenever we want – the list goes on. What they are really saying is they hate losing their independence. I learned firsthand how that feels this last winter.

Thanks to the last snowstorm of the winter and an insane but lovable (?) dog, I fell – hard. It was so easy—one quick slip on the ice because of being tripped up by my overeager dog. The result was a fracture of both knees, tears on both ACL and MCLs. In other words, I was helpless. I couldn't stand on my own, so even "simple" things like a trip to the bathroom was impossible without help. Thankfully, I had a lot of help. My husband slept on the couch outside the guest room door, the only bedroom on the main floor of our house. The stairs were out of the question. I felt trapped in that room, lying flat on my back with my legs elevated. You can only read for so long before your eyes complain. You are very aware of the ticking of the clock. Time slows down with your boredom.

Eventually, with help, I could stand long enough to get into a wheelchair. Freedom! I could go out to the living room! Once ensconced in a reclining chair, I had the TV remote to keep me occupied and the phone within reach. Still, my mood was less than perky. This turned out to be a 6-month recovery – to the point I could walk by myself and, eventually, drive. I'd still have another 6 months until I walked with more smooth steps and a normal gait. What did I learn?

First, and perhaps most importantly, I learned to accept help. I was afraid to be an invalid, but that's exactly what I was. Others were there to help me – even when I resented needing that help.

Secondly, I learned that others would "do" things differently. My blessed husband did the cooking. He is not a cook, but he made the meals for us – including our granddaughter who was living with us at the time. The problem was that he cooked the same meals over and over and over. I'll never look at a pork chop again without reliving those months. But we had food; no one starved. Eyes rolled as the food was placed with care on the table, but we ate.

The cleaning ladies now appeared weekly. They also did the laundry, something new for them. They were big on bleach and hot water. Now everything is clean, with streaks where color once lived and some clothes are a tad tight – but everything is clean.

Third, and last, I learned patience on a level I had never known. When your recovery is microscopically slow, your fear is that it will never come – or if it does it will take forever. "Forever" in my case was a year. A long time, but it passed – slowly but surely.

I lost my independence for a long time, but I got it back again. Knowing that independence would come gave me hope. That hope isn't there for some people and I pray for them because accepting that is hard. I was afraid for a while. When you look at your foot and try to make it move but it doesn't, your fears race ahead. When you see yourself as a burden to your family, you fear losing their desire to spend time with you. When boredom overwhelms you, you lose sight of the good things to come – like wiggling your toes! Throughout my experience, I prayed for recovery, yes. But, more, I prayed for understanding. Why had this happened to me? I never got a really good answer to that question, but I think I got part. I always say that everything happens for a reason, but we don't always know the reason. Maybe I just needed to slow down. Maybe I needed to be more grateful for the loving people around me. Maybe I needed to learn to love pork chops? Whatever the reasons, I treasure my ability to stand, walk, cook, GO! And I thank God every day for all the good things in my life.

Another experience from the coronavirus pandemic was the wait for testing results that Americans faced. Frustration over testing became nationwide. Once again, this is not new. Eileen has experienced waiting for the results of testing for a disease that other family members were exhibiting.

From Eileen: My mother's generation understood the threat of diseases. They had a high rate of infant mortality. Childhood diseases and illnesses like diphtheria devastated families in the 1920's-30's. In Mom's family, two children, ages 3 and 4, died of diphtheria. Two of her siblings survived the epidemic and lived to maturity. They married and together the three siblings had seven children. Growing up, the cousins saw each other almost every weekend at our grandparents' home. We were very close, even after living on opposite sides of the country made visits infrequent.

My cousin, Pat, was in an accident nine years ago. As she recovered, she noticed muscle weakness she hadn't experienced before. When the diagnosis finally came almost a year after her accident, we were shocked to hear that she had ALS, sometimes called "Lou Gehrig's Disease". There is no cure. She now had only the movement of her head.

Two months ago, my cousin, George, an avid golfer, noticed a weakness in his grip. The initial diagnosis was a pinched nerve. Eventually, that changed. Lou Gehrig's Disease had struck again. While the path of Pat's disease moved like a glacier, George's progressed like an avalanche. In a few months' time, he first lost the use of his hands and arms, then it moved to his feet. His family is hurrying to refit the house to accommodate a wheelchair, hoist and hospital bed – all on wood floors which require the removal of carpets.

So, of the seven cousins, two have the disease. Since there are two forms, one random and one genetic, the question for me became – am I next? They say that ALS hits most often between the ages of forty and seventy. That was true for Pat, but George was seventy-four. The only way to know if you carry the defective gene is to go to a neurologist and ask for a DNA test. Some of my cousins don't want to know. They argue that, since there is no cure and, basically, no treatment, why go through the testing? I don't see it that way. I need to know. Have I passed it on to my children and grandchildren? Or, has this cup passed us by?

I visited my family doctor and told him this story. DNA is the only way to know, so I got a referral to a noted hospital for testing. I had to wait two months for an appointment. Three days before, I was notified that there had been a staff change and my appointment had been rescheduled for four months later. Frustration. Worry. Naturally, I monitored every ache as a possible warning of the arrival of ALS. And nothing will change the number of days to wait. And, unlike what you see on TV, once the testing is done, the wait for the results is months, not days.

So, what have I learned? I am not nosophobic. A long time ago a wise man told me, "The past is history. Tomorrow is a mystery. Today is a gift. That's why we call it the present." I intend to open my present every day and enjoy it to the fullest. When worry sneaks in, I'll go back and remind myself of those words. And pray for the result I want and my purpose to be accomplished. Unless carefully managed, a physical disability can become a social and emotional one that cripples more than the actual illness. How I handle my illness becomes under my control.

As a side note, the test results are in—after six months of waiting. I do not have to worry about this illness. Illness does not have the last word.

This reminds Brenda of another womanly fear. Her least favorite annual check-up, but one she totally advocates—is the mammogram. Women don't exactly fear a mammogram, but women know it is not a visit that shows up as a happy place on our calendar.

Due to having dense breast tissue, Brenda has faithfully had annual mammograms since she was forty. Dense breasts are a breast cancer risk factor especially after menopause. Furthermore, statistics say that 70-80% of breast cancer patients do not have a family history of breast cancer. Earlier, Brenda had congratulated herself that breast cancer did not run in her family. Almost every other type of cancer did occur in her family, but breast cancer did not. Now she knows it is not always familial. There went that false reassurance!

Most women can relate. Upon arriving at the Mammogram Center, you are advised to put on the non-flattering hospital gown which is usually a jigsaw puzzle of getting the arm holes to align. Then the little sign in the dressing room requests that you remove your deodorant with easy-to-open pads. This seems counterproductive to remove deodorant for an office visit that causes a cold sweat. When your name is called to enter the examination room, you find a technician who apologizes for cold hands. You exchange glances. You know and she knows she is going to mold and mash your floppy (no longer perky) breasts into a flattened pancake. No need to smile for this camera. But you are requested to hold your breath and not move while your dense breasts are compressed beyond your imagination. So far, it is tolerable. You tell yourself it is not so bad.

It gets worse when you are told there is a suspicious mass. Now the mind games begin and the irrational fears. While you wait for your sonogram, you start composing your "what ifs." You have other plans, other places to go, with no time to be bothered by cancer. Your mind fills in what a mess this could be because you know the routine. You have friends who are breast cancer survivors or friends who did not survive.

The sonogram is painless, but the waiting is not. After mentally rearranging your schedule and composing your brave announcement to your family and friends, your stiff upper lip is starting to ache in a strange smile. Is that pity in the eyes of the other women in the waiting room? Yes, we all have a big imagination. Fortunately for Brenda, a sonogram has resulted in a diagnosis of "ok but needs to continue monitoring." Others with dense breasts have had to have biopsies. Brenda has faithfully followed the consistent mammograms and monitoring.

These are the examples where Eileen and Brenda know there are irrational fears, and our imagination runs rampant about our health. As Mary Pipher says in "Women Rowing North," "I could hardly go to the library or gym without running into peers who had just lost someone or heard alarming health news about themselves. I realized that during my healthy days, I had taken so much for granted. My questions about my health issue shifted from "Why me?" to Why not me?" I had envisioned all the negative possibilities—decrepitude, dependency and a gradual deterioration of all that truly mattered to me—but I realized the long view can be a perilous one to take. None of us knows what will happen in our futures, good or bad. It is much more adaptive to focus on building one good day at a time."

However, ignoring a problem, a fear, or a symptom does not make it go away. Second opinions are always a good option. Brenda's father had non-Hodgkin's lymphoma forty years ago. The disease was not well known and the first doctor that he consulted recommended surgery to "remove the lumps" in his arm. A second opinion explained these were lymph node lumps and to operate would have spread the cancer over his body. It would have been the wrong solution. Under the guidance of the second opinion, her father gained remission and survived 40 more years, living to be 91 years old. A second opinion is a very wise move.

Currently friends of Brenda have discovered health issues due to diligence on their part of seeking specialists in an intelligent and proactive way. But the point is that all of us have quirky fears and fearful moments with going in for a health check. As Dave Berry said, "I become faint and nauseous during even minor medical procedures, such as making an appointment by phone." It is only called a minor medical procedure when someone else is having the procedure. In your mind, your procedure is major!

Remember "If it is important to you, you will find a way. If not, you will find excuses." Excuses abound. Don't let a quirky fear keep you from being proactive with your health.

Let's Discuss

1. If we wait for the perfect time to go to the doctor or dentist, it may be too late. Can you give an example?

2.Maybe it is time to take a second look at my medical choices and see what they are based on? Proactive or avoidance due to fears?

3. As Eileen learned, illness brings uncertainties and loneliness. There is a partner in this journey. God holds the power not only to sustain but also to heal. Isaiah experienced this healing. In Isaiah 38:16-17 "O Lord, by these things men live, and in all these is the life of my spirit. Oh restore me to health and make me live! Behold, it was for my welfare that I had great bitterness; but in love you have delivered my life from the pit of destruction, for you have cast all my sins behind your back."

Have you experienced this partnership in health fears? Can you give examples?

Chapter Ten: Hakuna Matata: No Worries

How do the geese know when to fly to the sun? Who tells them the seasons? How do we, humans, know when it is time to move on? As with the migrant birds, so surely with us, there is a voice within, if only we would listen to it, that tells us so certainly when to go forth into the unknown." – Elizabeth Kübler-Ross

Not a single person is immune to the fear of the unknown. Yet when we watch television, a favorite movie or flip through a magazine, our imagination is caught by pictures of faraway places with strange sounding names. That little inner voice wants to live it, taste it, and reach out for newer and richer experiences. Yet, unlike the migrant birds, we remain seated on the couch. Getting to yes in a land of no is often our own decision making in overcoming our fear of the unknown.

Getting in charge of our fears may seem like a foreign travel experience. It is unfamiliar and out of our comfort zone. But we have God's assurance that we prosper if we go where He sends us. These little forays out of our comfort zone may build our self-confidence.

Is a vacation good for us? Yes. St. Augustine said, "Seeing the world is like reading a book and those who do not travel are reading only one page." If the experience of travel enriches us, then what are these fears that are holding us back? One suggestion for gaining self-confidence would be to travel in a foreign country.

Overcoming the fear **of being out of our comfort zone** can enhance confidence. For Brenda, a solo trip to Zambia followed by a safari tour in Tanzania was the most adventurous that she had been. Unfortunately, the car driven by her tour guide broke down. Brenda as a solo passenger had been admiring the countryside on the way to her first night hotel. Looking out the window, she saw tall Maasai boys who shepherded the sheep. They presented a colorful sight, wrapped in their red cloth.

While her tour guide opened the car hood to examine the problem, she got out of the van to take in the air, view the sunset and admire the wide expanse of countryside. The car was soon surrounded by helpful, tall Maasai adults who suggested elephant turd would help the leaking radiator. A child came up to her. Then the child admired her watch and in a loud voice suggested that she give it to him. The adults turned and reprimanded him. She decided she should get back in the van.

Finally, long after dark, the tour company sent another van to speed her on her way. The hotel had held her food for dinner, but the clock was ticking. Finishing her dinner at 11:45 PM, a hotel bellhop appeared to escort her to her room. She thought that was nice but unusual. He was carrying a rifle. To her surprise, the "room" was a picturesque outdoor permanent tent with netting around the living room and bedroom.

As he walked her down the path passing numerous permanent tents, she heard a distinct roar. Well versed in "Hakuna Matata" she said," Isn't that a lion?" "Oh, yes," he said, "but it is not close at all. I must caution you, however; you are not to go outside your tent during the night. You see, the elephants walk down this way and that is more of a threat than the lions. And by the way, all lights and electricity go out at midnight."

In the next few minutes Brenda dived under the covers in the dark and did not stir until it was daylight. The rest of the trip was wonderful, viewing the Serengeti and large herds of zebras, giraffes, elephants, wildebeest, and cats of all types. To this day on Facebook, her guide keeps in touch. However, that first night was not in her comfort zone. Safety in numbers remains a primary safety rule for her. Being a single on a safari, she admits, did allow her to see large numbers of animals free and wild in the Serengeti and unforgettable African sunsets. It made her realize she had the freedom to go where she wanted, even though she was single.

Eileen, too, has lessons on comfort zones. She says: It's ironic that culture shock takes place in reverse. Coming back to the states was as shocking as arriving to live in Rome. My mother-in-law was determined to get us to "admit" that America was "better" than Italy. Is that like apples are better than oranges? The best lesson I ever taught my children was that "different" wasn't a bad thing. After all, vanilla can be boring. Enjoy each new day and learn what you can from the experience.

This really became obvious to me in what I would call "Jan's last day."

For one of our first assignments, we lived in military housing in Frankfurt, Germany for a little more than 3 ½ years. The quarters were apartments in three story buildings with three stairwells per building. At the center of these buildings there was a Department of Defense Elementary School. These buildings were lovingly referred to as the American Ghetto.

From the time we got orders to Germany, we made a conscious effort to experience as much of European life as possible. That wasn't easy, given Joe's long hours, our limited funds and having 2 preschoolers, but we did it. The language was a problem because of our limited resources. A language textbook and best wishes were the most we could manage on learning German, but that didn't stop us.

Early on, I made regular trips to the local German supermarket. Shopping in the Commissary meant lower prices, but the local market had truly German food. Wursts and other lunch meats were reasonably priced. The bakery was a treat for the senses. The fact that we were trying to learn was well taken. Pointing and holding up fingers worked fine. Elderly customers would stuff my children with jelly doughnuts and refuse payment.

My friend, Jan, lived in the apartment above ours. She and her husband took us along on day trips to small villages along the Rhine. Our children were steps and stairs in age and got along well. Finally, it was time for them to move on and, custom was that you fed the packers. (It kept them on the job and prevented long lunch breaks.) Jan asked me about shopping in the local market. She'd never done that before and was nervous. She didn't speak German and didn't know about the measurements. I assured her that she'd be fine – just point and hold up your fingers and you're in!

When I saw Jan returning from the store in tears, I could have kicked myself. I should have gone with her. What could have gone wrong? That was my question to her as she came closer. Why was she so upset? Her answer shook me. She said that the people were very kind and helped her get the order together.

They insisted that she try each item then and there to be sure she liked it. And it was all wonderful. And it was Jan's last day. There wouldn't be any return trips to buy wurst or cold cuts. No trial tastes to make sure it was OK. Go home to the states and get the same things all the time at the deli. She had missed her chance.

That was a big lesson for me. Don't miss the chance – to try a new food, take a new class, visit a new place, learn a new language, experience a new culture. There are so many things to try. I still remember Jan's last day each time something new comes my way. It may be out of my comfort zone, but it's worth a try – and I do. When God gives us opportunity, we need to step out on faith.

Brenda can echo this. Doing international consulting for Christian non-profits means the blessing and the learning has been on both sides of the equation. It has been growth-enhancement.

Brenda says: One of my first mission trips was to teach at Russian American Christian University in Moscow. The flight to Moscow on Polish Airlines was satisfactory, but they seemed to take their flight instructions from hospitals— interrupting sleep at every opportunity. Even the flight departure card was hard to decipher. It was written in Russian. Russians often say that if Moscow is the face of Russia, the countryside is the heart. Helping with an orphanage in Syzran, I took the train from Moscow over the 600 miles of countryside to Syzran. You do not get a choice on persons who share the over-night sleeping compartment with you, so it was suggested by Russian friends that a single woman traveling alone should purchase a two-person compartment and lock the door. My Russian friends helped me purchase the ticket.

Naturally, when the ticket collector came, she had an interesting twist. She said yes, I had paid for the compartment. However, that was for the trip, not the use of the bed. I am not sure how a person can buy a compartment, but the price doesn't include lying on the seats. I am sure that she was telling the truth because she brought her white uniformed, muscled matron to explain. I paid an additional fee because if the matron sat on me, it wouldn't be pretty. On another summer trip, I taught at a Christian University in St. Petersburg. I brought my granddaughter Skylar along with me and she hopped on and off the Metro in St. Pete like a pro. We loved St. Petersburg, but I must admit that I took Skylar home via a stopover in Paris. Paris stole her heart. With a gleeful smile on her face as we walked toward the Eiffel tower, she tugged my arm and said, "Gram, someday, I'm coming back!!" Riding the French metro, we leaped off to stroll in a shopping area that the concierge had assured me was the best place to shop. Concentrating on the shop windows, I had not noticed the pedestrians walking in front and behind of us. My granddaughter tugged my arm once again and said, "Gram, I think we are in a walking parade." It turned out that we had merged into the Gay Parade that was going to wind up at the Bastille. It was a colorfully dressed crowd. We decided to take the tourist route back to the Metro, the Eiffel Tower and our comfort zone. Paris remains one of Skylar's favorite cities.

Due to work schedules, I have very favorite memories of summer trips consisting of three-week teaching assignments. The students at the University of Guilin in China explained to me that they must carry my books and protect me from the summer sun with their umbrellas since I was their professor. I taught a summer session in Lehza, Albania, Tbilisi, Georgia, Lusaka, Zambia, and my favorite of all, Klaipeda, Lithuania at LCC International University. Sometimes these also included consulting assignments for giving business seminars. These short international assignments and travel remain my favorite growth enhancement because it requires that we step outside our comfort zone and build confidence.

Eileen admits that having lived in Italy for part of her husband's career gives interesting insight.

By the time we got to Rome, we had teenagers not toddlers. Language was something to overcome, and my daughter and son did so with style. Although there was the time that Brett needed to buy food for his Boy Scout camp-out. He practiced

"I need eggs" and came home with grapes. What's a vowel here and there? For Brigid, it was the magic of attending a newly co-educational high school. It was every mother's dream, to have a daughter, one of 13, amid 100 boys.

This also recalls how much fun Brenda and I have when we travel on our adventures. One time we went to Poland to finish research on my ancestors. Brenda and I drove to the back of beyond from Warsaw, arriving in Strekowa Gora. Throw a stone and hit a Russian, very close to the border. There we were in our rental car, on a "road" that was really a manure path, in the rain, going downhill with a loose stone wall on one side and a cliff on the other with no place to turn around. Either go straight ahead to God knows where or back up. We backed up as I spoke mentally to every long dead ancestor, asking for some help. It must have worked because, in what seemed like an eternity, we pulled into a level clearing. There was an old woman there watching the crazy Americans. I got out and tried to speak to her, but her hearing was bad, and her sight was worse. Two days later, we returned, after having searched the Church archives and having found my family's history.

Brenda was determined for me to find a living relative. She said she had prayed about this and was going to try. She started knocking on doors. Finally, we found teenagers who spoke English and they took us, by way of the village busy body, to my ancestors, still farming in the same place as my grandfather had done so long ago. It was a woohoo moment! It was also a stone's throw away from that manure path. God had sent us to the right place, we just didn't know it.

It's possible that I would have found the data in some other way, but what could have been better than sharing the experience with a good friend – one who was willing to make it an adventure?

Sometimes the adventure of travel takes strange turns when the family has different ideas of "ideal" and "educational. "A memorable vacation for Brenda's family was the time they went to Disneyland which they renamed Dizzeyland for all the mazes of line waiting. Being the only female in the family, of course, Brenda chose a side trip to Hollywood. The males in the family were not so sure about this idea.

Brenda said: Naturally the first stop of the tourist mecca is Mann's Chinese Theatre so we could compare footprints with the stars. While there, we decided on self-guiding ourselves through the neighborhoods with a "Map of the Stars Homes." With a big grin the Iranian girl assured us that the Guidebook she was selling was updated. Hot on the trail, we sailed down Sunset Strip and Hollywood Blvd. Hmm, left on Oakhurst, the home of Shirley Jones. "Who's she?" echoed from the back seat. The closest I could do was describe re-runs of the Partridge Family. This Guidebook was not current.

We zoomed along. After all, my husband was the driver of this tour. We passed the "former home" of Elvis and Priscilla. Even though the home had probably had several occupants since then, I noticed a zealous Elvis fan had printed, "Elvis reigns forever." Thinking of the occupants forever hassled because a home had once been occupied by a star, I had my first pangs of guilt for this stargazing trek.

There was a little more excitement from the guys when we buzzed by Pickfair Mansion. At that time, it was the home of Dr. Jerry Buss, owner of the Los Angeles Lakers. Owner of the Lakers was a much better status than movie star. Now turning on Roxbury Drive, a street infested with stars on our guaranteed map, we have a Star Line Tour bus pull in front of us and stop. All eyes on the bus turn to stare at the house. "David," I wail, "that must be someone **current** as they are not listed on our map." I hated not knowing whose house we were all staring at. Somehow this reminded me of the moose jam in Colorado when tourists slammed on their brakes to peruse

119

some mild-mannered moose, placidly chewing grass. With that, we abandoned our Guidebook and I readjusted to what mothers of sons could enjoy.

Driving over to Malibu beach, we found my sons much preferred jumping out into the sand and trying their hand at volleyball. Unfortunately for me, I was innocently standing on the beach when a Muscle head strolled over to say, "Sorry, we were practicing our spike and I lost it in the sun." He lost it. I found it. His volleyball had smashed me in the side of the face and broke my sunglasses. He declined of course to pay for my sunglasses with a "Ma'am, it was an accident," as he strolled away. Oh well, so much for rose colored glasses of Hollywood!

Hakuna Matata. No worries. The path that God sends us on may seem like a foreign experience. It is unfamiliar and out of our comfort zone. But we prosper if we go where He sends us. These little forays out of our comfort zone may build our self-confidence and lessen our fears.

"For my thoughts are not your thoughts, neither are your ways my ways, says the Lord. For as the heavens are higher than the earth, so are my ways higher than your ways, and my thoughts than your thoughts. For as the rain comes down, and the snow from heaven, and returns not, but waters the earth, and makes it bring forth and bud, that it may give seed to the sower, and bread to the eater: So shall my word be that goes forth out of my mouth: it shall not return unto me void, but it shall accomplish that which I please, and it shall prosper in the thing where I sent it" (Isaiah 55:8-11).

Why don't we do this? We often kid ourselves that we don't have the time to pursue our dreams. It is called procrastination. To be a healthy human is to want to be challenged and to grow. The mental stimulation of learning a new skill or trying something different in your career takes a good deal of thought and energy. The rewards are worth the effort.

Don't make excuses--make a list. List all the obstacles that are holding you back. Talk to your support system — your spouse, friends, family — about how they could help as you begin to work on something from your list. By saying it aloud, we are making a commitment.
There is more help with this in the next chapter.

Let's Discuss

1. Jesus was very patient with the disciples in their misunderstanding and slowness in His ministry. Often it was like foreign territory. Have you acted or even tried to act with that same patience in dealing with others who are unlike you?

2. Can you give some examples where you have moved out of your comfort zone and experienced some interesting or rewarding travel?

3.The Pharisees were indignant with Jesus because he sometimes dined with sinners. When we are indignant over someone's behavior, our reaction is often because *our* dignity has been offended. That's a mistake. That's what the

Pharisees forgot. That's what we need to remember. Have you allowed the fear of imperfection or something being too different to keep you from travel?

4.We could be Simon the Cyrenian. Jesus had said, "*If you want to be my disciple, take up your cross and follow in my footsteps.*" Simon was pulled from the crowds and without even knowing why, he suddenly was forced to carry a crossbeam across his back. He literally walked in the footsteps of Jesus. We may not know why we have been given this cross (just as Simon didn't know), but we may be asked to follow in the footsteps of Jesus to foreign territory outside our comfort zone. Can you think of an example?

Chapter Eleven: Fears Here, There and Everywhere

"The angel of the Lord encamps all around those who fear Him. And delivers them." Psalm 34:7

In summary, let's be honest! We all have fears that disturb us due to overactive imaginations.
We have gaps caused by these fears between where we are and where we want to be. Our bodies look like *this*; we want them to look like *that*. Our careers are *here*; we want them to be *there*. A relationship is *dragging*; we want it to be *soaring*. Our children see our *mistakes*; we want to be *heroes*. We need to *eat more vegetables*; we eat *fast food*. We want to Instagram our picture after counting calories. We drink a diet drink; we finish it off with a cookie.

Sometimes we can't bridge these gaps because we don't know how. At other times we know *exactly* how to bridge the gap, but we still can't seem to make it across.

Fears are contagious—to our children, and to our friends. Have you ever noticed on a bumpy airplane flight how you take your cue from the flight attendants? If they continue to walk about and talk normally to passengers or even if they take a seat but remain calm looking when an air pocket occurs, you feel somewhat calm and release your tight grip on the arm of the seat or the unsuspecting passenger next to you. However, if the attendants exchange glances with each other in that "knowing" look, your fear escalates. And you get to know your neighbor up close and personally.

The Lord is aware of our fears. *"Have. . .wisdom. . .and common sense. . .With them on guard you can sleep without fear. . .for the Lord is with you, he protects you."* Proverbs 3:21, 24-26. There are over 100 Bible verses telling us not to be afraid. To paraphrase this last verse, with good common sense and wisdom, you can sleep without fear for the Lord is with you.

Even Paul the Apostle in Romans 7:15 admits that what he wants to do, he does not always practice. He sometimes does what he doesn't want to do. As humans we know that we cannot escape from the valley or the "ups and downs" of life. When Brenda was in Israel, she saw the deep Valley of the Shadow of Death. She had no idea that there was an actual Valley of the Shadow of Death. She had thought it was a metaphor for the end of life. She could now actually see the barren, rocky, huge mountain of boulders as a desolate place for David to be running for his life from King Solomon. As a psalmist, David questioned, he agonized, he became angry; he was disobedient and despondent. But he never lost sight of who God is.

Brenda and Eileen especially like the 23rd Psalm," *Even though I walk through the valley of the shadow of death, I will fear no evil, for you are with me; your rod and your staff, they comfort me.*" Eileen and Brenda know that it does not say, even though I walk *around the shadow of death.* We are all going to go *through* shadows. That phone call, that email, that doctor's visit may bring unwanted news. We all know this is a part of life, which doesn't make it any easier. Yet, we can know that God wants to walk with us. It is instinctive to sense His presence. When we are in the dark, we look for the light. You can't live in the shadows if you face Sonshine. Then, your shadows are behind you. We can't change our past, but we can change the stories or assumptions we tell ourselves about it.

Brenda recently attended a church service/conference that talked about living in the shadows. It was a Church service/conference presided over by Mrs. T. D. Jakes at the Potters House in Dallas. Most women in the audience were survivors of Sex Trafficking. (This is the transportation of persons by coercion or deception into slavery-like conditions.) It has been said that two-thirds of U.S. trafficking victims are US citizens, mostly women and young children. The top three states with the most human trafficking are California, New York, and Texas. The Dallas/Fort Worth area produces 30% of the trafficking in Texas. Trafficking survivors know fear, physical and mental. This fear has kept them in the shadows from very young ages. Shame and stigma have often kept them from education and the prospect of earning a full-time stable job.

Many of the survivors who spoke on this panel gave help, strength, and encouragement. Sometimes they had been trapped in trafficking at the tender age of six years old. The panel of survivors with total agreement could state that we all have the promise of His presence, His power, and His protection. *"Fear not, for I am with you; Be not dismayed, for I am your God. I will strengthen you, yes, I will help you, I will uphold you with My righteous right hand."* Isaiah 41:10.

We can choose even in the most difficult situations to be fear-conscious or power-conscious with our God.

Escaping from the previously mentioned extremely fearful situations is hard to imagine. But the audience was full of survivors who were determined to turn themselves over to the Lord to gather strength from Him.

Richard Carlson has said in his book <u>Don't Sweat the Small Stuff</u>, that "Life is a process, not a destination. It's not like you are going to "get somewhere" and all will be well. Instead, joy is in the path itself. Your journey is the day-to-day, moment-to-moment process and the attitude that you bring to that path has everything to do with what you will receive along the way."

There are merciful and positive ways to think about others and us. We can question even our most painful experience to see that, indeed, we did have resilience and worth. We can hone our skills in reframing the story we were telling ourselves and question, "how did that make me grow stronger? Was the fear rational or irrational that held me back?

On a visit to Rome, Brenda saw the actual hole in the ground that was the Mamertine prison that Paul spent the last days of his life in. She had pictured a cave-like prison where people could freely move around. However, this underground small hole left Paul in total claustrophobic darkness with clammy dirt and boulders. The room was accessible by climbing two floors down in a hole in the floor. It was closer to a sewage tank than a prison cell. This would be enough to strike fear in the strongest heart. Yet Paul was able to write to the Philippians from this prison cell, *"Don't be anxious about anything, rather, bring up all your requests to God in your prayers and petitions, along with giving thanks. Then the peace of God that exceeds all understanding will keep your hearts and minds safe in Christ Jesus."* Philippians 4: 6-7

There is a thought, that if you live in the past in your mind, you will be living with regret and possibly be controlled by depression and past fears. If we live in the future, we live with anxieties about what might happen, and we live in worry. But if we live in the present, we can feel the joy of being fully engaged in the moment and the presence of the Lord that gives us peace.

We cannot control life situations, but we have complete control over our actions. We can train ourselves not to let irrational fears define us. Our mistakes, traumas and regrets are there, but so is our joy and strength that we can tap. We do not know our capabilities until we try.

Eileen and Brenda are now giving you a structured activity or sensory anchoring. This is the important key to <u>Fear, Cracked open</u>. This is the key statement to getting rid of fears that are holding you back. We want to move you to the second part of the book in discovering your purpose. Here is the key point:

What gives you the ability to do something big one day is the discipline to do something small daily and consistently.

Let's explain. As humans, we underestimate the power that slight changes can make big differences. Simone Biles has taken her place as one of the world's greatest gymnasts. She did the unheard double twist and double somersault on a bar and then did a triple twist and double somersault on the ground. It took a million practices to perfect each small move that led to this accomplishment. Golfers make small changes in their grip to get the greatest drive. Those who want to lose weight must make it through those first meals and then have the discipline to consistently follow through. Those who want to save their marriage must go to that first counseling session. Running a marathon begins with a run around the block. Again, *what gives you the ability to do something big one day is the discipline to do something small consistently.*

Research has shown that successful people consistently do what most others only do occasionally. Successful people do the 99% that only 1 % of the population does consistently. Too often, we **fall** to the level of our habits or comfort level, rather than **rise** to our goals.

So, here is the homework. Think of two to three things that if they happened this next year, you would count the year as a success. Then, fill in the blanks with those 2-3 things in the sentences below:

What will give me _____ (an example of success or something to achieve)

Is the daily discipline to _____(a small action to be taken)

Then, what are some fears that are holding you back from achieving this? What disciplined actions would it take to face that fear, ignore that negative voice in your head and act? Are you opening another door because one has closed? Has life given you a detour?

Has a set-back really been a set-up for something good?

Where do we want to be? Soaring with the eagles, not stuck with the turkeys. Our hearts are restless. No lasting change of our fear happens-- until the pain of staying the way we are surpasses the pain of the change process for getting over fears.

As a change management consultant for corporations, Brenda learned when pain is high enough, and hope is strong enough, you will change. Otherwise, you find. . .excuses.

How would we act if we were 100% convinced that God is part of the conversation? We wouldn't be crossing our fingers for magic. Faith overwhelms fear. Trust transforms.

Jesus demonstrated this early in his ministry. He and his disciples took a boat over to the other side of the Sea of Galilee. *"A furious squall came up and the disciples woke him, "Teacher, don't you care if we drown?" He got up, rebuked the wind and said to the waves, "Quiet! Be still!" Then the wind died down and it was completely calm. He said to his disciples, "Why are you so afraid? Do you still have no faith?* Mark 4: 37-41. Aren't we all guilty of being amazed when Jesus calms our fears or handles the situation? When He returned in His resurrection in Acts, they were at last convinced they could trust Him with their fears. They stepped forward on a journey to witness to the ends of the earth.

Are you ready? Can you release past fears and come into the present with God's help by your side? Can you get clarity over confusion? Faith over fear? Prayer over panic? Each stage of our life brings change where we must redesign or decline.

We vow to become a new, improved version of ourselves. We want to change our circumstances. We were not ready for this new stage! We don't want to have to change ourselves; **we want You, Lord, to change our circumstances, not us**! Reality can trounce our dreams or plans.

Three examples of athletes who made spectacular failures are Shaun White at Sochi, Lindsey Vonn in Vancouver, and Dan Jansen at Lillehammer. The whole world watched as an elite athlete, crashed and burned. Shaun, Lindsey and Dan all crashed only to come back stronger and win the gold at the following Olympics. And you wonder, "How could they ever make a comeback?" It is discipline with perseverance. It means small changes with consistent discipline instead of imagining the worst. They didn't quit.

The Bible is full of stories of people who had epic failure. For example, David was a national hero, but his life spiraled downward as he grew older. He arranged the death of his loyal general so he could steal the general's wife. How did he rise from this disgusting low point? He got up, washed himself by scrubbing off the old, and changed his clothes. He went into the house of the Lord and worshiped. He didn't change his circumstances but changed his outlook with small changes and consistent discipline (and a much cleaner smell as well as outlook).

Before we rush over and take showers, here is the zinger. Have you ever thought that *what you are on the inside determines what you achieve on the outside?*

In other words, we become mired in the daily routine of "should and would." We cannot allow visions of "should," anchored in the past, keep us from what "could." No matter what our life stage is, we can learn to grant ourselves permission and to make intentional choices.

Chapter Twelve: The Master Plan

Once we have recognized our fears, what do we envision for our lifestyle? What is our purpose? What do we hope to accomplish in our latest stage of life? How do we redesign?

Why are we making this choice—did we choose it or someone else chose it for us? Are we in daily survival mode or making headway towards what we really want? Who will be there with us on this journey? If we look into the mirror, we may reflect some images that we have been ignoring. Maybe we should look twice!

Once we have reached different life stages, we notice an important thought. Each decade brings the need for new assessment due to new circumstances. New hopes, new dreams, and often a new purpose invade our plans due to life's changing circumstances. Some directions we would not have chosen, but life intervened.

Oprah Winfrey has been on a Vision tour with influential trailblazers and changemakers. She has said, "There is no greater gift you can receive than to honor your calling. It's why you were born. And how you become most truly alive."

Most of us would raise our hand and say, "Yes! I want to feel truly alive!"

OK. So here is THE big question. How can we know what our calling is? We have likes, dislikes, abilities, and passion. Society may agree or disagree with our decisions and choices of trial and error. One of Oprah's friends, Reverend T.D. Jakes has said, "If you can't figure out your purpose, figure out your passion. For your passion will lead you right into your purpose."

Eleanor Roosevelt said, "One's philosophy is not best expressed in words; it is expressed in the choices one makes."

Eileen and Brenda believe that we have a model to share with you that will help answer the dilemma of finding purpose for our life as a new life stage has been dropped on us. This is not limited to the super-spiritual. We are writing for the wobbly and weak kneed who know they don't have it all together.

Progress is messy and perfection looks all put together on the outside. All of us are present. Not perfect. As we look at the life of Jesus, a life development model has four steps.

First, you must discover your **identity**. We will explore how identity comes from early decisions, as well as family, physical, mental, and spiritual influence. Eileen interjects that our identity is not always what you expect, but sometimes it is what others perceive. She remembers answering the door and a neighbor's child asked with all sincerity and big wide eyes, "Boomer's Mommy, can Boomer come out to play?" She gulped. At that point, she had not thought of her identity as being the mother of a dog. Boomer was her dog.

When Jesus grew in wisdom and stature, he understood his identity as the Son of God placed on this earth. By the age of twelve, he was telling his parents that he must be about his Father's business. But he did not start his ministry until he was thirty. There is a clue in this.Typically, as impatient humans, we want to jump immediately from our discovered identity into our mission and purpose, thinking that we have found our calling.

Forward, ho! Or "Ready, fire, aim!" But if we look at the Bible, once we have success, it is inevitable that trials will follow. You think you've got it and then comes a clunker! These trials are what we are calling the "**wilderness.**" In truth, the wilderness teaches us what God would have us do, because that is when we finally listen.

Therefore, the second step is that our identity will be followed by an inevitable **wilderness**. This happened to Jesus and to us.

After Jesus was baptized, the wilderness followed. After Paul discovered his identity on the road to Damascus, he too experienced the wilderness. As Paul said in 2 Corinthians 4:7-10, "We are hard pressed but not crushed, perplexed but not in despair, persecuted but not abandoned."

Paul was in the dark. He was struck blind. Even after he came to understanding and his sight returned, he retired to the wilderness to rethink and re-evaluate his former life before starting his ministry. This is the dark side.

Our life is not all sunshine and lollipops. We struggle. We suffer. None of us jumps out of bed in the morning and tells ourselves that today we are going to willingly choose a hard pressed, perplexed, and persecuted day. Our life stages have an inevitable struggle. There is purpose to the pain. This struggle helps our human minds understand that God is in control.

The **wilderness** makes us stop and listen to that still small voice. If we didn't have the hard, how could we appreciate the easy? By gaining self-awareness, our soul can expand. What counts is the effort we put into knowing ourselves.

For the Third step, Jesus emerged from the wilderness. He immediately selected and surrounded himself with a **community**. He selected his twelve disciples so that he might have men to teach and carry on his earthly work.

However, he also selected men to share his heart, humor, and well- being. Paul also selected friends like Timothy and Titus who could share his burdens and joy and perpetuate his message. Through his friend Barnabas, he gained the trust of the Christian community. His friend Barnabas had the trust of Christians which opened the way for Paul to talk to them.

Consequently, this is the Third Step. The value and importance of friendship and **community** for self-development is not to be overlooked.

Finally, girded by a sense of **identity**, strengthened by the **wilderness** testing, and supported by a **community** of friends and disciples, Jesus was ready for his **mission/purpose**.

We believe this four-fold development plan will work for you. Intrigued? Let's continue in the next chapters.

Chapter Thirteen: the Land of "er"— prettier, smarter, thinner

"We do not dare to classify or compare ourselves with some who commend themselves. When they measure themselves by themselves and compare themselves with themselves, they are not wise." 2 Corinthians 12.

When we talk about discovering identity, my mind travels back to when Brenda and I first met. It was February of 1969.

It was a time of adjusting to a new **identity**. Brenda and I had both graduated from college and were newlyweds. Added to this, we were about to learn not only what it meant to be a wife, but to be a wife in the military. As the saga began, my husband, Joe, and I returned from our honeymoon, packed our worldly goods (which consisted mostly of clothing and wedding presents) and set out for Fort Eustis, Virginia.

Upon arrival, I was both frustrated and frightened when we were informed that there was no available housing. We were given a list of motels from Newport News to Williamsburg. It was a variation of "no room at the inn" as we made our way from place to place going further and further from the Army post. It got darker and darker. I didn't know it then, but God was directing us to the last place on the list – the Tanglewood Lodge in Williamsburg. That was where we'd meet David and Brenda Shull and form a lifetime friendship.

The day had been totally frustrating. Military life did not seem like what I expected. Or married life either. We had our first quarrel that night. Joe was insistent on emptying the rented U-Haul and returning it in the next thirty minutes to avoid an additional day's fee. I was insisting on putting things in their proper place with extra steps and organization (and time). Plus, this new efficiency apartment was tiny and there was no place to walk.

Totally frustrated, Joe stood at the door and announced, "If you don't like it here, why don't you go back to New York?" At that exact moment a booming voice interrupted our glaring exhausted frowns. "Now leaving on Track 2, the Greyhound special to New York City." Wow! What a lovely neighborhood. We then discovered we had a bus terminal in the back yard sending out advice. Let's just say, exhausted giggling broke the tension. It was the beginning of a new identity and way of life—complete with bumps and booms.

The next morning, Brenda and I met in the parking lot while waving off our husbands to their new adventure in Officer Training. Although Brenda and I had many things in common, I think it was the differences which were more interesting at first. We both were English majors with minors in Secondary Education. We were both recently married, both nearly the same age. We both had husbands who, due to the Viet Nam War, were unsure of their futures. We were both far from home, living in a motel complex along with other military families who were on TDY (Temporary Duty) assignments.

The differences? They were geographical, and religious. Growing up in a predominately Jewish neighborhood, other than my fellow Catholics in a new, small parish, I thought of Protestants like an exotic species. I had a lot to learn.

Part of the new identity included the skill of cooking. Brenda knew how to cook. I was a beginner. My mother was probably the world's worst cook. My mother collected cookbooks, but to her, it was fiction. This was not a Julia Child role model. I was still at the stage where the food looked and smelled "done" but was raw inside. We referred to those dinners as "Previews". Sometimes dinner was served at 10 P.M.

From Brenda: One of my first startling discoveries about Eileen was her creativity in cooking. I was truly amazed when she led me to her bathroom so I could glimpse a frozen turkey swimming laps in her bathtub. She had the water on high which forced the bird into bobbing laps. She felt it was the quickest way to defrost the bird she planned to bake that night. It probably was.

And of course, she gives my cooking expertise too much credit. I came from the era when high schools had recently deleted "home economics" and crammed the schedule with advanced math and science courses for college bound students. Fortunately, I was allowed to add "Choir" to my electives. My mom asked what I was going to do since I only had science courses when my future husband looked for dinner. I answered that I would sing, "Let's go out to eat." Through the years I developed quite a repertoire of that song and verse!

My mom could not really judge me. She was not a cuisine queen. She thought making a dessert "from scratch" was sliding your polished fingernail under the lid of Betty Crocker brownies mix. She said Betty would not pay those engineers to create the powder if it weren't a good idea.

However, Mother insisted that I "practice" a few meals during high school to get some standby recipes. This also relieved her from cooking dinner. Unfortunately, this means my poor dad was the recipient of my beginning cooking efforts. Often when I proudly presented dinner, my dad bravely maintained his sense of humor. Patiently he cut into a slightly bloody chicken. Taking tentative bites, he remarked that this chicken wasn't cooked. It was just overwhelmed by the heat.

In later years I compensated for undercooking. When my sons were playing outdoors, they often knew that dinner was ready because the smoke alarm went off. I, of course, believe it was just an overly sensitive smoke alarm. As the boys grew older, I noticed that dinners might take an hour to prepare but would be consumed by the three boys in 12 minutes. Half time of football games on television takes 12 minutes. This was not a coincidence.

Eileen, on the other hand, progressed to becoming the excellent cook she is today. My identity is not associated with gourmet food. I currently ignore the kitchen. I go by the belief that the kitchen just happens to come with the house. One of my built-in ovens is still a virgin. I once considered cooking lessons while in Italy, but my son Justin said that would be a total waste of money. I took it anyway. The Italian recipes (still untried) are firmly entrenched in my kitchen drawer should the need arise.

Cooking, however, was a sub-set of our new identity. Sitting next to each other at our first orientation meeting (naturally it wasn't called orientation; it was a "tea" with refreshments), we found we had been thrown once again into the "Land of er." Comparisons of prettier, smarter, better were being peppered into our thinking.

We exchanged glances. Yes, I remembered a few years before when I arrived for sorority rush at The University of Texas. I saw other fledgling freshmen who nervously glanced at prettier, smarter, richer girls. Would you believe that Farrah Fawcett (future Hollywood star and she looked it!) was one of the freshman lovelies standing in the "rush" for a sorority? However, those first nerve wracking days of comparison where someone always was prettier, or cleverer had faded into the familiarity of a large university with room for everyone.

Now in a new life stage and adjusting to the identity of the newly married officer wife, the "er" was back. This is a repeating pattern.

The stakes had been raised. We were informed that a social mistake could "rearrange your husband's career—a young officer's efficiency evaluation included an analysis of the wife."

Eileen and I exchanged glances again. Politely but blatantly, we were informed that an officer's wife could make or break an officer's career. Both of us felt pride in our young husbands' duty for the freedom of our nation. Here at the tea, we were patted on the shoulder to be told that as a junior officer's wife," it was easy to be overawed by the rank around us" and we "would feel a glow when you know you are tastefully dressed." "In a dinner dance, a long skirt, long gloves, and jewelry would add to this glow. A fur stole would add a note of elegance." I mentally pictured my mother's mink stole, stashed several years before in the moth balls.

"Wearing a hat to make a call," although not required, "signifies the importance you place upon the call and is a sign of respect to the senior officer's wife." The quotations are direct from the 1969 Handbook that we were given at the beginning of the meeting. At this, Eileen muttered quietly to me, **where** is the red lipstick? Is this "I love Lucy?"

We felt we had fallen twenty years behind into the 50's.

I had to hold my breath to keep from laughing out loud. I had just been picturing Jackie Kennedy Onassis and how her bowl hat did **not** look good on me, so my chances of dazzling were not good. Eileen and I realized we were being given a new identity in a mental time warp where an invitation for an official luncheon was a command performance. We were told

140

"Teas, like luncheons, are feminine. This is when your quarters should sparkle, your tea table the prettiest you can devise and the food the daintiest you can serve."

It was once again the Land of **er** where comparison trumped contentment. Somehow it seemed counterintuitive that one result of Officer Wives Club is "a more interesting, better-informed wife for your husband to come home to." Juggling and fretting over the size of the correct calling card on the Army Post made Eileen and I question in which century we had landed. Naturally, we wanted the best for our husbands. It was a surprise adjustment to a new identity in the land of "er."

So, let's discuss the idea of identity. Identity is a complex mix of influences, from the womb and the world. We get identity from family, friends and the forces of our environment. Eileen and I were suddenly thrust into some revealing moments of a new identity as a Army wife in the 1970's. Our new environment encouraged reshaping into a more competitive mode that surprised us.

So, let's discuss. How about you?

1. Have you had an identity forced on you that was not by your choice? Was it a new role and society's expectations? How did you adjust?

2. Have you been surprised by the identity of "wife" or "single" and what is a lesson learned?

3. Have you landed in the land of "er"? Does your identity and self-image suffer because you are busy comparing yourself? Did you discover that there is never contentment if you are constantly living in

141

comparison? How have you changed from the land of er? Or are you caught in it?

In comparing ourselves, we start to look down on others. We may even boast. Paul says: "For it is not the one who commends himself who is approved, but the one whom the Lord commends." 2 Corinthians 10:18

Let's examine **identity** further.

Chapter Fourteen:
The Good, the Bad and the Better Not

The Bible is clear that Jesus was always confident of who He was and why He had come to earth. From our glimpse of Him at age twelve, until the end of His life, we find Jesus confident of His person and message.

His parents went to Jerusalem every year at the Feast of the Passover." *And when he was twelve years old, they went up to Jerusalem according to the custom of the feast. When they had finished the days, as they returned, the boy Jesus lingered behind in Jerusalem. And Joseph and his mother did not know it; but supposing him to have been in the company, they went a day's journey, and sought him among their relatives and acquaintances. So, when they did not find him, they returned to Jerusalem, seeking him. Now so it was that after three days they found him in the temple, sitting amid the teachers, both listening to them and asking them questions. And all who heard were astonished at his understanding and answers. When they saw him, they were amazed; and his mother said to him, 'Son, why have you done this to us? Look, your father and I have sought you anxiously.' And he said to them, 'Why is it that you sought me? Did you not know that I must be about my Father's business?'* Luke 2:41-49.

From this account we see that at the age of twelve he was listening to teachers and asking them questions which surprised them due to the depth of his understanding. As he began his public ministry, His confidence in His calling was sure. He told the religious rulers exactly where He came from. *"You are from beneath; I am from above. You are of this world; I am not of this world"* John 8:23.

John the Baptist knew. "The next day John saw Jesus coming unto him, and said, Behold the Lamb of God, which taketh away the sin of the world" (Jn. 1: 29) In conversation with the Samaritan woman who mentioned the coming Messiah, Jesus said, *"I that speak unto thee I am he"* John 4: 25, 26.

Consequently, how do **we** find our identity?

Technological shifts have caused paradigm shifts from the culture around us. When Eileen and Brenda were children, we used a rotary dial telephone (that is an apparatus completely unknown to young readers). Today our children speak to us via Apple Watches on their wrists. Or they text us with memes as soon as they can get their toddler hands on the phone. Today our phone can ring on the mountain top, exotic desert or in the depths of the grocery store. Of course, this phone call is probably a robo-marketing call from India. Not only has technology changed, but cultural shifts have shaped our thinking.

Our identity is constantly being pelted by society's perceptions. How fortunate for us, during change, that neither God nor our basic needs have changed. "For God hath not given us the spirit of fear; but of power, and of love, and of a sound mind." 2Timothy 1:7.

Eileen and Brenda can point to the change in society's perceptions for our identity as women. The coulds and the could nots in the early 70's would surprise the young women of today. It was a time of the good, the bad and the better not!

The unstated but understood goal of college for most girls in the late sixties was to get a M.R.S. degree, sooner rather than later. Brenda's mother's friends questioned her not being married at 20. The median age of marriage in the 60's and 70's was 20.5 years. This is compared to 27.1 years for American women and 29.2 years for American men, currently.

A young woman would be coached by her friends to keep her mouth shut—for two reasons. One reason was not to break the rule of being smarter than her date and two, not to French kiss or "go below the waist" without serious sexual consequences. Until that time, America had been a country where abortion was illegal. Roe vs Wade legalized abortion in 1973 which once again initiated change. Now, it has changed back.

Girls had to be shorter than boys, so hunched shoulders added to the adolescent droop. College sports were off limits for girls in those days (even intercollegiate teams were only for males). We sunbathed on the dorm rooftops using Baby Oil and Iodine to get a good tan (before we knew of cancer risk). A few sorority sisters smoked cigarettes and a few copied Holly Golightly in Breakfast at Tiffany's smoking with long cigarette holders (before we knew of cancer risk). Others took up smoking while playing bridge or at fraternity parties. But the number of smokers was not like the numbers today who are smoking or vaping at younger, middle school ages.

There was a definite difference in career choices for identity in the late 60's and 70's. Typically, career choices were limited to two choices: teaching or nursing.

Translated, this meant salary potential was limited to a teacher or nurse salary at about 20 cents on the dollar to what male salaries were. Therefore, credit cards were issued in the husband's name. Brenda remembers applying for a credit card in her name and being turned down because she did not make a high enough salary as a teacher. She could obtain a credit card with her husband's supplemental income, or she could receive a credit card if she put the card in his name. It is shocking now to think women could not get a credit card unless their husband co-signed.

The University took steps to help remedy career choices. Brenda remembers sitting in a selected audience in an auditorium at U.T., Austin. The sole purpose of the convocation was to encourage the selected females in the audience to attend law school. At that time, less than 10 percent of females were in law school. Today medical and law schools throughout the U.S. female enrollment equals more than 50%.

Getting a job after graduation was another story. In a prestigious law firm or bank, you might be passed over because it meant displacing a Viet Nam vet. A typical interview question that Brenda personally was asked was if she planned to start her family in the next five years and did her husband agree with her going to work.

If she answered yes to starting a family or that her husband didn't want her to work, the interview was over.

One distinguished female law graduate at U.T. (who later became a U.S. Senator) had a difficult time. With law degree in hand, it was rumored she had to settle for becoming the Weather woman on a local Austin television station since law firms were reluctant to hire a female.

Law firms assumed a female would only get pregnant and leave the firm after a year or so. This is verified by a 60's Harvard survey of law firms that gave a negative rating of hiring females because "Women can't keep up the pace." "Responsibility is in the home" as stated by these law firms reply on the survey. Further, the law firms were "afraid of emotional outbursts."

It is documented that some of the extraordinary women rejected early-on by major law firms were Rep. Geraldine Ferraro, Fordham University, 1960, Attorney General Janet Reno, Harvard University, 1963 and Sen. Elizabeth Dole, Harvard University, 1964. These ladies later distinguished themselves in Congress.

One friend ventured into the exciting world of computers. In those days a computer's physical size took up the entire bottom floor of a building, unlike slim line laptops today. With trepidation, the employee would feed the punched cards into the computer. If a punched card had gotten bent or out of order, it would be a total rewrite and another late-night run. My friend remembers watching engineers throw chairs in anger if their forced late-night computer-runs were unsuccessful. After an unsuccessful run, my friend was chastised because she had quietly gone back to her desk with her head down and without any display of anger. But tears had trickled down her cheeks. Her manager said the men couldn't handle seeing her with tears so she must not cry. The emotional outburst of throwing a chair was excusable. Tears were not. This company was a very well-known Big Blue computer company, and these were the early years of women in the technology workplace.

In 1970, Brenda attended graduate school at the University of Delaware. She was among only a handful of female graduate students in the English department. She was told that she was among the first women accepted for the graduate school in English. Looking back, it is hard to believe. At the University of Delaware there were less than 20 female professors of tenure-track, mostly in home economics and education departments in 1970. Women were not allowed to eat in the faculty dining room. Brenda was an adjunct faculty, so she never attempted the faculty dining room. Pay inequity was rampant with two-tier level of benefits, including vacation, sick days, and health insurance. The female co-eds were forbidden from smoking or staying out past curfew in the dorms of this "co-educational "university. With wit, gumption and a wily charm, Mae Carter ultimately would help lift UD into the forefront of the then little-known field of "Women's Studies," which today enjoys broad acceptance. In those times it was openly mocked by some male faculty, who said to Mae Carter's face that they hoped Women's Studies would fail and advised her that it was tenure track suicide. (Just as an update: in 1993, 12 percent of the UD faculty were female professors. In 2019, it stood at 30 percent as published in a UD bulletin.)

Whether in law firms or the hallowed halls of a university, female role models were hard to find in professional careers. By 1990, Brenda had decided to return to The University of Texas, Austin to get her doctorate while she worked full time at a job in Fort Worth. She chose to write her dissertation on "Critical Incidents in Leadership Development of Women." It is a subject near and dear to her heart. And a reflection in this book.

From Eileen: Quite rightly, Brenda talks about the changes of identity in society during those early years when we first met. Career identities have evolved.

My first job interview following graduation from St. John's University was with American Airlines. Arriving at JFK Airport, I saw one of my fellow graduates interviewing with the airlines. I knew it had taken an act of God to get this guy through the university. He was not the sharpest knife in the drawer. I had a surprise when we finished the interviews and required testing. I was surprised to hear that he had been offered a managerial position.

Despite excellent grades and a strong interview, I was given the choice between airline "hostess" and passenger service representative, or as it was then called "pisser." I chose "pisser." I had the difficult job of eight hours of walking in high heels throughout the airport helping angered passengers with travel issues.

All the while, appearance was everything. A run in the stocking or not enough lipstick would send you to the floor supervisor to ask for permission to have a bathroom break to change those stockings. On the job training took various forms whether it was using a sultry voice to announce international connections or tolerating a grope.

In my actual experience, a grope on the escalator by a supervisor was justified as a "love handle check." While traveling down the escalator, a supervisor joined me on the narrow step, to quickly sneak his arm around my waist and hug me to him, squeezing my side. With a grin he said, "Love handle check", smiled and leaped off. I was supposed to be flattered.

Now in the Army as a young wife, I remember being told that purchasing a copy of "What Every Army Wife Should Know" was a requirement. By shelling out $3.85, I could learn in fourteen chapters what I could, should or shouldn't do to keep my husband's career afloat.

Luckily, I "could" teach – it was an acceptable employment. I "couldn't" open a bank account on post, get a Library card, or cash a check without listing my husband's rank, position on post, and Social Security number. To this day, I can rattle off Joe's Social Security number without hesitation but am slower on my own.

In those days, getting a job if you were married to a military member wasn't easy. The question always came up – how long will you be living here?

Questions now considered to be illegal were fair game back then. In the past three years was the absolute maximum for an assignment, it didn't matter how wonderful you were, you weren't "permanent".

The only time that didn't matter was when I was hired to teach in a parochial school near Harrisburg, Pennsylvania. The Pastor accepted my application. As he said good-bye, he commented that it really didn't matter how long I stayed because he couldn't afford to pay me a "living wage". Lucky, I worked cheap.

Driving through strange neighborhoods became the rule because we moved so frequently. It was constant immersion in new homes and communities. Learning to drive had been no easy task. I had learned to drive in a standard transmission car, with power nothing. In Queens, New York, there wasn't much open space for new drivers. Large parking lots at shopping malls were the only places for practice, and then it had to be after hours, in the dark.

My Mom had taught her sister, brother, soon- to- be- husband and cousin how to drive. She said it was in self -defense because she was the only driver when they went on vacation and, when she became ill on the way, no one could take the wheel. Otherwise, they had to wait until she felt she was able to drive and continue their trip. The result was a group driving course when they reached their destination.

When I was finally able to take the test, I found out that the road test was given on the Van Wyck Expressway.

For those not familiar with this neck of the woods, it's the massive highway which connects John. F. Kennedy Airport with the other major roads in and out of New York City.

As in so many events in life, it was a case of sink or swim. I swam. I've been swimming ever since – through Rome, Frankfurt and the outskirts of Warsaw, mostly on the right-hand side of the road.

Identities and "could and should" have changed for women. These examples have probably surprised the younger women. We can't change the historical social perspective of the past, but we can emerge and flourish by reframing. We can hone our skills in perspective taking, emotional processing and not paying attention to cultural stereotyping of what someone in our latest stage (old, young, married, single) should do.

Let's Discuss. What do you think?

1. Obviously, as we walked down memory lane, we see historical cultural norms have changed. What are some of the historical culture norms that have shaped your identity?

2. Have times changed? Sexual discrimination in job interviews has lightened. Have you experienced this? Has this affected your identity in your career?

3. With recent developments of the MeToo movement and Time's Up, there have been movements against sexual harassment. Can you see an improvement and has this affected your identity?

4. Jesus was very certain of his identity. God had a plan for his life. Jesus based his understanding on God's Word. Have you been searching for God's plan for your life by examining your identity and looking in God's Word?

Chapter Fifteen: Pull Up Your Big Girl Panties

"Home" is a strong component in our identity. Did your family give you a basic security—a structure of stability, shelter, and nurturing? Did your parent(s) give you admiration—a genuine feeling that you were worth plenty in your own right? Did your parent(s) give you warmth and physical affection, cuddle and hold you? Research has proven the value of cuddling and loving touches. Did your parent(s) accept you, right or wrong?

Sadly, your earthly parent (s) may not have given you this support. Your Heavenly Parent does. Are you aware that your Heavenly Parent values you and wants a good relationship with you?

*"How lovely is your dwelling place, O Lord Almighty .
. .Even the sparrow has found a home, and the swallow a nest for herself where she may have her young—a place near your*

altar. . .Blessed are those who dwell in your house; they are ever praising you." Psalm 84: 1-4

Part of our identity comes from our home environment. As adults we now can create a nurturing home environment for our family. As we start our families, whether as dual parent, or single parent, we must decide if we want our nesting place to be perfect, beautiful, and/or a place to "be." Early on, Eileen and Brenda realized they had a proclivity to being active joiners. Yet, both have tried to achieve a balance.

They tried not to fall in the trap of a "human doing" but a "human being." A perfectly managed home, correct in every detail and relationship, never made it to their immediate neighborhood. In their mind, perfection is a sure sign of someone who doesn't have enough to do. Eileen remembers her mother's standard of housekeeping was somewhere between "House Beautiful" and the Board of Health. The cleanliness of her and her oven was between her and God. She did not fall in the trap of comparison in the land of "er" --- clean*er*, shini*er*, bright*er*.

Eileen and Brenda's home life (and life stage) changed with the advent of children. From being a fertility patient, Brenda became immersed with three boys in diapers (ages 3 and below). Watching three active boys, she saw the concepts of Sunday School being interpreted by preschoolers. Her middle son would race over to the youngest boy and swipe a toy. To justify swiping a toy, he would announce in a large voice, "God wants us to share." Fortunately, the youngest just shrugged and thought his big brother was lots of fun.

In the meantime, her oldest son was introduced to Mexican food at lunch after church. While dipping his chip in the salsa, he quickly looked up. Derek questioned, "If Jesus lives in my heart, won't this salsa burn him?" Sunday School was doing its job. Brenda wasn't sure that she was.

Eileen and Joe, however, had quite a different concept of "home." They continued in their professional life of military with moves to Rome, West Point and Middle America. With multiple moves, Eileen had to establish the identity of home no matter where that might be.

Eileen states: The idea of "home" varies from person to person. My ancestors made their way from Europe to America in the 1800s. They were proponents of the theory of growing where you are planted. Once here, they never moved more than a block or two from their first homes for seven generations in New York. Joe and I were the transplants.

I observed early on that many military families who live away from family and old friends often speak of the place they came FROM as "home". For the most part, they were always ready to go "home" as soon and as often as possible. It made the time while they were living away seem intrusive and unpleasant. They were always counting the days until they went "home".

I decided after observing this reaction to make "home" as part of my identity wherever we lived for however long we lived there – a season, a year or longer. Granted, I didn't unpack the Christmas ornaments if we were moving in October, but I did more than hang the pictures on the walls. I knew that it was important for my children to see our time in this new and unfamiliar place as an adventure to be enjoyed – and that "home" was where we lived together as a family. In summer, we had one day a week devoted to the interesting things to see and do in this new place. A zoo, a park, a museum, a tourist stop – we did them all. We were walking tour guides when it was time to leave. Sometimes we returned when Joe was reassigned to the same town. The challenge then became finding new places to see and things to do. It prepared us for our own guests' visits – we knew where to go!

Our trips back to visit family were never as frequent as we would have liked, but it was the best we could do with the time and money to make them happen. We were once visiting my in-laws when our children were preschoolers. We visited every place where my mother-in-law spent time and were introduced to endless friends and acquaintances. When we finally returned to her house, she explained to the kids that life wasn't "fair". Her friends had their grandchildren close by, but she was being "cheated" because we lived so far away. I sat there, not sure how to respond to that. Before I had decided what to say – or to just keep my mouth closed (a more difficult choice), my 3-year-old son took her hand and said, "Nana, other kids have their grandmas near where they live, and their visits aren't special. But when we see you, it's like a party! It makes your visits very special." My mother-in-law never brought it up again. While she wasn't thrilled to be "taught" by her grandson, she couldn't argue with his logic.

I can't say I loved each place we lived. One still makes me shudder as I remember it. But I can say that God showed me how to live in each new place. He guided me, so my children wouldn't feel like gypsies, but adventurers. It tightened our family and gave us resiliency – far more than I would have thought back in Williamsburg, Virginia, when I first met Brenda.

To this day, my kids say they "hit the ground running"! They don't wait around to see if they'll be asked to participate in some activity. They introduce themselves and start going. Still, my daughter confided in me a while back, the hardest question for them to answer at a party or gathering of strangers is "Where are you from?" (People want our identity). She was born in Savannah but left when she was one year old. She's our

Georgia peach in a bowl of Big Apples – everyone else was born in New York. She attended five universities for varying amounts of time, but she got her degree! "Sticking to it" should be her motto and I believe it is part of the attitude she got from "home."

"Home", therefore, is a very strong component in our identity. Are you giving your family basic security, no matter if you move often, or have single or multiple children?

Don't worry, no earthly parent can score 100% on their parenting. If this is your life stage, you can make a difference in the home that you are currently establishing and in the identity of your children :

"How lovely is your dwelling place, O Lord Almighty . . .Even the sparrow has found a home, and the swallow a nest for herself where she may have her young—a place near your altar. . .Blessed are those who dwell in your house; they are ever praising you." Psalm 84: 1-4.

You have the help of a heavenly Parent in establishing a good identity for your young ones.

How about you? Let's Discuss

1. Is a firmly established identity of "home" with a sense of wellbeing part of your identity? If not, why not? How has "home" shaped your identity?

2. Mothering is powerful. Mothers can transmit a different culture. What if women paid attention to what they wanted and moved with confidence and joy toward their deepest desires? Is your **altitude** defined by your

attitude of "home"? What is a step you can take with confidence toward the establishing the home of your deepest desire?

Chapter Sixteen: The Multiple Demands on your Identity

"Train up a child in the way he should go; even when he is old, he will not depart from it." Proverbs 22:6

There is such a diversity of identity found in "motherhood. This life stage deserves more discussion.

Specifically, your identity as a mother has different demands if you have an all-girl, all boy, single parent, dual parents, twins, mixed gender, special needs, and large-spaces-in-age family. If your identity or life stage is "Motherhood," the wide diversity brings different demands on your identity.

Brenda's role turned out to be the mother of three sons. She had grown up in an all-girl family. She liked shopping, education, and more shopping. She had to adjust to an all-male environment. Have you noticed that little boys don't walk on the sidewalk but wander to the curb or climb whatever obstacle happens to be beside the path. While walking with her grandsons, David and Jackson, she noticed the same choices that their dads made—a simple walk became an adventure in climbing, throwing rocks into the lake, stumbling on an unsuspecting squirrel and hopping just for the fun.

Being the only female in the three son and husband family meant a different vacation than she had experienced in an all-girl family. Hiking, golfing, attending sports, and some camping replaced shopping. It meant "active" vacations. Fortunately, the redeeming quality of camping was that other members of the family agreed that cabins rather than tents were the way to camp. None liked the sunrise in sleepy eyes and grungy feel of morning dew when waking up from hard sleeping bags..

Brenda remembers: With three energetic boys, we hiked and then fished in the mountain lakes and streams. Usually, a competition would ensue over who had the best walking stick. Derek would find a 6' stick and whittle on it, then Justin and Vance would argue over who got Derek's last walking stick. We would hike, but it could only be called "safe" for the animals. With Justin and Vance knocking the trees with the sticks, there was no way we were sneaking up on any bear or unknowing elk. With great zest we examined the trail for bear scat or bear hair—often it was Spanish moss, but it made a good thrill. The boys would get their fishing license and fish in Colorado or Yellowstone Lake for cutthroat trout. They also liked to sleep late. Most fish aren't hanging around for 10 o'clock scholars.

Did I mention constant energy? When the fishing got boring, they would have a contest getting wet. "We were wrestling— He threw sand on me, so I pushed him, and he stepped in the water" said with a big smile. Justin would usually sigh and say, "This is fun, but I'd like to actually catch something." In later years we did fly fishing, but the results were pretty much the same. The finesse was better. We could see the trout and they could see us, but tree stumps, local reeds and low hanging trees got in our way. Frenetic motion, jabbing and laughing might have had something to do with it, too.

More fun was the whitewater rafting. For years this was on our agenda. Hooking toes under the front end of giant rubber rafts, then bumping on the rapids and turning sideways in a wall of water was fun. We always used an experienced guide. The boys loved the bucket fights with other boats where everyone got wet in the flat part of the river. The fourth year we thought we were good enough to do individual rubber kayaks on the white water. Big mistake for Brenda.

After a brief 5-minute introduction with instruction to "always hit the rapid straight on, not sideways," we were off. This is when upper arm strength pays off. Three strong boys and one strong dad all shot off ahead of me in their kayaks. I was muttering to myself "straight on, straight on." I made it through a few sets of rapids, but too soon the serious rapids came up. Thinking "straight on" but heading sideways, I soon flipped out of my rubber kayak. I knew to put my feet downriver as I shot through the rapids dragging my rubber kayak on my left hand and hanging on to my paddle with my right hand. I saw the guide in the far distance paddling toward me as I hurtled down the stream. Then I saw his eyes widen and he shouted, "Let go of the raft."

I saw what he saw. A treacherous set of boulders rose downstream. I was hurtling toward them. I thought to myself, "I'm supposed to be a smart woman, and I am absolutely doing something stupid right now." It was a little late to reconsider being in (or out of) a kayak. I felt a wall of water pour over my head which pushes you down. Then resurfacing, I felt my tennis shoes land with a thud against a boulder.

By reflex, I could push off from the boulder. It was a reflex, not because I knew what I was doing. This push forced me into the air and landed me in a peaceful side pool of the river. The guide paddled his way over to me and I flopped onto the back bow of his kayak, waterlogged but extremely happy. Let me repeat that, extremely happy, to be sprawled on the back of his kayak like a beached whale.

Meantime, down river, another guide said, "Ooops, we lost someone." My sons and husband looked around, and Vance said, "Where's Mom." It was the first time they had noticed me missing. The rapids had been demanding.

I was re-assigned to a group whitewater raft with older patrons for the rest of the trip. It didn't hurt my feelings one bit as I turned in my paddle. To this day I like to go whitewater rafting. I even went this last summer—with a group and a guided raft. This doesn't mean that I did not thoroughly enjoy the outdoors and adventures of being the only female in the family, but it created a different identity from my "shopper" female friends with daughters.

Eileen says: While there are differences in style, there isn't a difference in content when it comes to raising sons and daughters. I am the mother of both a daughter and son.

Likewise, my daughter is a very independent person and has always been so. My lessons have continued as I have met my daughter's daughter. With girls, you really can't focus on self-image. This idea on self-image became clearer to me when I took my granddaughter to see "The Nutcracker" at age four. At that age she had never seen live theatre before. Joe had arranged for seats on the apron of the theatre. We were so close that when the dancer's sweat flew, it blessed us. She was mesmerized by the entire experience. At intermission, I asked her what she thought, expecting to hear a comment on the costumes or a kid answer about how pretty it was. Instead, she looked at me intently with a very serious expression. "Nonna, I COULD do this." It was a statement of pure fact, not opinion. I patiently explained how these people had studied for years and she would have to take ballet lessons. She was ready at that very moment to join them on stage. She did take ballet lessons the next year. She disliked being told how to dance and not just move creatively with the music and the moment. In her mind, her self-image of dancing across the stage with grace and charm was much stronger than following a pattern of steps told to her by someone else. How sad that we stamp out a child's creativity and replace it with cookie cutter images of beauty. The irony is that Flynn has taken that creativity and moved it into music as a songwriter and singer. Having recently celebrated her "sweet sixteen" birthday, she is going to a songwriter camp at Berkley this summer.

Of course, Brenda got a different response when she took her eldest son at nine years to "The Nutcracker." At intermission, she leaned toward him and said enthusiastically, "What do you think about the fabulous leaps of the dancers?" To which he replied, "Yes, now I know why they call it "The Nutcracker."

What about you? Let's Discuss:

1. In discovering your identity, how is it affected by the gender of your children?

2. Have you had a whitewater moment where you questioned your sanity and got in over your head? Has your identity perception caused you to get in over your head?

Much of our self-image comes from our childhood. Our childhood patterns then persist in adult choices. How has this affected your identity?

Chapter Seventeen: The Wilderness: the "proof" is in the pudding.

"Our fathers disciplined us for a little while as they thought best; but God disciplines us for our good, that we may share in his holiness. No discipline seems pleasant at the time, but painful. Later, however, it produces a harvest of righteousness and peace for those who have been trained by it." Hebrews 12:10-11

And so goes life. We know that life is full of change and the unexpected. We think we have it planned. We have examined how our **identity** has come in focus through society's perception, our environment and culture. Our life stage affects our identity. We are rocking along. Suddenly there is a bump.

Life is life. We are either having a problem in our life currently or we are going to have a problem. As soon as Jesus announced his ministry, He was sent to the wilderness for 40 days. As soon as the Jews escaped from slavery in Egypt, they were sent through the wilderness for 40 years. Have you noticed there is a pattern--a **wilderness** experience is often a metaphor for our darkest experiences in life? This wilderness seems to come soon after a success or a new plateau in our life stages.

The wilderness stage either slows you to a stop or prepares you to emerge stronger.   In our earthly life, our parents discipline us to correct our behavior. In God's hands, what would hurt His children instead deepens spiritual roots and produces new fruit. There is purpose in the pain. Brenda's daughter-in-law Melody sent her an encouraging magnet for her refrigerator. It said: a woman is like a tea bag. The hotter the water, the stronger she gets.

This testing in the wilderness calls believers to draw nearer to God. We pay attention when the going gets rough.

The wilderness awaits. One of the great mysteries of God is His ways. Sometimes when we get in the most difficult places, it is as if God were indifferent to our circumstances. It appears that He is turning His head from our sorrows. In the Old Testament, Job said, *"Yet when I hoped for good, evil came; when I looked for light, then came darkness"* (Job 30:26). When we go into these dark periods, we often begin to see light that we never knew existed. We might not have discovered this light or truth if life were simple. The truth is that we only want to be rescued. None of us like the **Wilderness** experience. Yet God has told us countless times that He will never leave us.

There is a purpose in the **Wilderness** experience! When we look at a map of Israel, it is amazing to learn that the 40-year ordeal for the Jews who were led by Moses to escape slavery in Egypt could have been a three-week journey via the mileage.

When we go on to Deuteronomy 8:2, *"Remember how the Lord Your God led you all these forty years in the wilderness, to "humble you", and to "prove you", in order to "know what was in your heart", whether you would keep his commands."*

There it is. If you do not allow God to humble you and reveal to you the issues that are in your heart, you may not be ready for the Purpose or Mission that you are looking for in your life.

The Children of Israel did not do these specific humbling and knowing their heart. Instead, they murmured and complained and despite several chances, they never changed. The first generation died in the wilderness. Yes, they were saved from the hands of Pharaoh, but a generation died without obtaining the promised land that was given to them by God. Only Caleb and Joshua along with the next generation were ever able to cross over and keep the promise that had been given. They had passed the test.

Have you ever thought when you are going through a dark wilderness experience that this might be a 'proving ground'?

It is where we must stay until we get right with God. Then, He allows us to truly possess the Promised Land and start working on our purpose in our new stage of life.

Let's check our model with the life of Jesus. We see that after He was baptized in the river Jordan, the Spirit of God came upon Him. Immediately the Spirit of God drove him in the wilderness to be tempted and tested (the proving ground). Satan offered kingdoms, riches, and power. Jesus understood. He humbled himself. He responded to Satan by quoting scripture. Jesus was in the wilderness just like the children of Israel, but instead of 40 years, it was only 40 days! He passed every test.

He did not exalt himself because He was the Son of God. (He knew his identity). Secondly, He did not misuse the power of God that was within Him and remained humble. Third, He proved that He was not going to worship another God.

God knew his heart. After God examined his heart, the scriptures tell us that Jesus came out of the wilderness (the proving ground) in the power of the Spirit, selected his disciples (community) and began his ministry (purpose). He deepened his spiritual roots and produced new fruit in a new stage of life.

As we depend on God's strength, He gives us the power to change patterns of thought, word or actions. We can use our energy in a new power over the hot water we have placed ourselves in or dark wilderness that we have stumbled on following our new life stage.

This is an important concept to grasp. The power of yes consists of affirming our own needs. Then, being assertive enough *with God's help* to leave that wilderness or any situation in which we feel neglected, discounted, or disrespected. We do not have to stay in the wilderness with His help and perhaps a change of our attitude in a new life stage.

From Eileen: Facing the wilderness isn't a favorite thing. Yet, challenges come at us every day. There is no hiding from them. The only thing we can do is to tell the truth to ourselves and move on.

The truth is often not well received, especially when it does not match what we want. The danger is not in talking about sore subjects. This can lead to just not talking. Ask God to help you and be ready to not necessarily like what He has to say.

There is an Irish saint by the name of Dymphna. She is the patron saint of some terrible things, like rape and incest, but the one that relates to me is "Dysfunctional Situations".

Sometimes I think my life is one long dysfunctional situation, so I speak to her every day. When Brenda and I were in London, Brenda found a lovely antique chandelier in a curio shop. She decided to buy it and have it shipped to her newly renovated home.

Was it possible, she asked, to wait for the shipping until she returned from her trip? "No problem", was the shop owner's reply. When she got home, no chandelier. When it hadn't arrived for a few weeks, she wrote to me and said she thought it was a lost cause. File it under the category "Lessons Learned".

I wrote back and told her to have a long conversation with Dymphna. The chandelier arrived with little damage and now has pride of place… in her bathroom.

I tell people about Dymphna because we all think that, at times, there are too many challenges in our hectic lives, too many problems to overcome.

The old saying, "This, too, shall pass" doesn't always apply, but knowing that you can have a conversation with God… or Dymphna, can make it more bearable. We have options. Sometimes it is the power of "no" with a burst of joy to getting to "yes!" I recently consoled my daughter Brigid, as she felt overwhelmed, that a conversation with Dymphna might be in order. The wilderness and changes in life stages are going to occur as we seek our Purpose.

Let's Discuss:

1. God intended for us to feel loved and have a deep inner knowledge of who we are and where we are headed in life. Can you think of a wilderness experience that has helped you?

2. Does it change your attitude toward your wilderness experience to think of these 3 things: to humble ourselves, to experience it as a proving ground, and to help the Lord see our heart?

3.While in the Wilderness, do not pray for tasks equal to your power. Pray for power equal to your tasks. What does this mean to you personally?

4. *Without faith it is impossible to please God*" (Hebrews 11:6). Do you know this peace that prevails?   When have you found the unexpected to give you peace that passes understanding in getting to "yes!"

Chapter Eighteen: Points of Light

"Consider it pure joy, my brothers, whenever you face trials of many kinds, because you know that the testing of your faith develops perseverance." James 1:2-4

John Muir, the naturalist and philosopher, has said, "Into the forest I go, to lose my mind and find my soul." In other words, it is not logic that we find in the wilderness experiences, but it can be soul food.

Thinking of John Muir, who first advocated our national parks, we are reminded that the Wilderness phase is easily compared to a hiking journey. To get through the difficult spots, we are huffing and puffing and probably complaining. To get through it, we place one foot in front of the other. More than likely, however, there is beauty to witness every step of our grumbling way. The beauty is not just at the summit, but along the way. And so goes our personal wilderness journey.

Sometimes getting away to a physical wilderness takes us out of the hustle and bustle of our daily life to give us a new perspective.

Being a city girl, Eileen had an interesting wilderness experience. She says: When my parents were visiting Newport News, Virginia, they asked about property values. They were about to retire and were considering a move from New York. I picked up a local real estate booklet and tossed it onto the cocktail table for them to see. It opened to a page listing six acres on the Hardware River. Never heard of it.

Long after they left, I looked at the listing. Where was the Hardware River? It was in beautiful Albermarle County outside Richmond. I mentioned it to Joe, and he suggested we take a drive over the Easter recess.

I called the real estate agent for directions who ended with "turn left at the tree struck by lightning and go to the bottom of the dirt road." We went!

It was spring and everything was in bloom. Flowers were everywhere. The "river" wasn't wide, but it was full of spring runoff and was moving rapidly. Paradise. But we were leaving for Germany in a few months. What would we do with this land? We came to the decision that we'd make a ridiculous offer. Surely, they'd refuse, and we'd be able to say that we tried.

They said yes. When we spoke to the realtor, she said that other than one Eagle Scout, we were the only people who had found the place! We managed to rent a camper and every chance we could, we went to "the river." These were special days. There was a huge rock where we'd sit and fish. We had a fire in the evening and cooked those tiny fish. Nothing tasted so good. But there was one problem—plumbing.

On our first adventure, we brought along a plastic training potty. That did not fly. On the next trip, on Mother's Day weekend, Joe presented me with a "camp potty." It was a folding "seat: with a plastic bag attached." It was an improvement, but still no privacy. Joe solved that issue by attaching an old Army blanket to a few trees. Brilliant!

When it was time to break camp, he moved the potty down to the bank of the river, out of the way of things to be packed into the car. He reminded me that the kids needed to use the "facilities" before our long ride home. Fine for them, but what about me? "Don't be ridiculous," he said. There's no one for miles in any direction." I did feel a bit foolish. I dropped my jeans and sat down.

Then, across the river, walking along the bank, I saw them. It was a pack of Boy Scouts walking in my direction. Quick. What could I do—stand up? Ignore them? Sing? Wave? Freeze like a deer in headlights? I decided to try to look casual—maybe I would blend in. Slowly. . .very slowly, the scouts walked along the opposite bank, looking at me with open mouths and poking others in the ribs and pointing. It seemed to take forever for them to pass. When they were finally out of sight, I felt free to stand and get put back together. Joe made the fatal mistake of shouting about what was taking me so long. What indeed. It was a long and very quiet trip home.

The next time we went to the river, a portable potty which could fit in the camper came with us. I never saw any more Boy Scouts after that. Maybe they were as embarrassed as I was. No, that's not possible.
A few years later, we were at a cocktail party in Germany. Folks were talking about their camping experiences. I shared mine. A man to my right asked a few questions about the

location of the property. I told him how the only store for miles was at the intersection of two country roads.

He smiled and said that he was from that area. He said, "Ma'am, do you know that you own a piece of Walton's Mountain?" Earl Hamner wrote his story about that place, changing the names for privacy. The store was "Ike Godsey's" general store in the book and later in the television series. We still own the land. Our son and his friends still make visits. Our plan was to build a retirement home there, but we ended up on our farm in Connecticut. We think, despite our earlier plans, God surprised us with our hearts desire in Connecticut. No regrets. Happy memories of a place that gets away from it all. And lessons learned about the need for privacy. And plumbing.

From Brenda: Most of the time, the Wilderness experience is not physical, but it is a life experience. As we discussed in the last chapter, the Wilderness phases of our life often feel like there is no light at the end of the tunnel. Or if it is a light, it is an oncoming train. However, even when we are in the wilderness and being tested, there are points of light.

Brenda experienced those points of light in the wilderness when her 52-year-old husband was diagnosed and being treated for A.L.L. (acute lymphocytic leukemia) at M.D. Anderson in Houston. Early in the diagnosis and following a bone marrow spinal test, he was not waking up.

Brenda goes on to say: David had the test that morning and I became concerned that it was now afternoon and he had not awakened from the sedative for the test. I kept pointing this out to the nurses coming in and out of the room until finally my persistence resulted in the floor doctor being called.

After examination, the doctor said, "This is a grave situation. It appears to be a subdural hematoma causing a coma."

Consequently, David started being prepped for surgery to drain the blood and pressure from around his brain. Time passed. It was now approaching midnight. The Department Head Neurosurgeon had been called in to do the surgery. I noticed the technicians were shaking their heads. Their body language projected the seriousness of the life-threatening situation. The shrug of their shoulders seemed very resigned to me as if they did not hold out much hope.

I just couldn't accept the discouraged attitudes that I kept observing in the medical prep. The anesthesiologist arrived to explain the procedure and possible standard side effects. Loss of math skills (David's job heavily employed the use of math) and loss of short-term memory were just a few of the potential negative side effects from the coma. When he finished the long list of potential side effects, he asked if I had questions.

He was surprised by my question. I said, "Yes. David is 52 years old. He chooses to live. Are you prepared to give this surgery your **absolute best effort** so you're at the top of your skillset? He wants to live." The doctor was startled. But he stammered, "Yes, of course." When he left, my sister-in-law Fran, a nurse, was sitting with me. She began to chuckle. She said doctors were not used to that question. I knew, however, that David chose to live. I could not accept giving up or having less than the best effort on the part of anyone.

I returned to David's darkened hospital room to gather his things because I knew he would be sent to intensive care following the surgery. The room's walls seemed to be closing in on me, becoming narrow and claustrophobic. For the very first time I admitted to myself that David might not make it through the leukemia.

It felt dark and lonely as if I were at the bottom of a pit. Then, behind me, I honestly felt energy surging toward me. I turned

175

around to see a doctor who stood at the door and was rocking back and forth on the balls of his feet with his hands clamping together in enthusiasm. The light from the hospital hall poured into the darkened room and seemed to surround him so I could barely see his face. He said with a smile, "I am the doctor who will be doing the surgery. I wanted you to know I am ready and at the top of my game. I just stopped by to let you know."

By 3 AM David was out of surgery and in recovery. I watched my three sons who had driven madly in the night from both U.T. Austin and Dallas. They were each holding David's hands and foot as he blinked awake. David greeted one son, adding multiple sums in his head verbally to tell Vance that he had just deposited some money in his college bank account.

He greeted Justin to talk about football plays in the U.T. intercollegiate team that my son was quarterbacking. He then greeted Derek inquiring about the crazy midnight drive from Dallas. In other words, his math and short-term memory were intact. About that time the smiling neurosurgeon walked in. Something that was attached to his collar flickered in the light. For the first time, I could clearly see this glimpse of metal reflecting the light. It was a small silver cross on his collar. A point of light in the darkness.

What about you? Let's Discuss:

1. We want the Garden of Eden, not the Wilderness. When we are taken into these dark periods, we begin to see light that we never knew existed. As you look back, have some of your wilderness periods been illuminated by newer spiritual eyes?

2. When have you faced self-doubt about your decisions? Have you felt direction from God? If you don't listen, you don't hear.

3. Sometimes God is pruning us. A gardener prunes to encourage fruit. Has God pruned you and did it bear fruit? Have you noticed that a gardener's hand is never closer to the plant than when he is actually pruning the fruit? Have you felt His Hand while being pruned?

4. How well are you suffering in a manner that is _unlike_ the world of non-believers? Instead, do you suffer with hope? Will you pray for hope when quick, earthly solutions cannot be found?

    When courts do not deliver justice? When evil people seem to get ahead at your expense?

    When an illness is not curable? We have a faithful Father.

    Have you lost hope or do you recognize the source of help?

5. Are you angry, frustrated or surprised at God for a past loss or present struggle? Jesus's death looked like a failure. Will you pray for the courage to believe, by faith, that God's plans are perfect?

 Chapter 11 in Hebrews tells of historical men and women who obeyed God's call to live by faith in Christ alone.

They confronted immense challenges in their days to carry forward God's cause.

They overcame hardships with joy because they believed God is faithful to His promises.

 Some are well-known biblical heroes; others are unknown to us, but God knows all of them well.

Have you thought of God's promises that may be just around the corner?

Chapter Nineteen: Onward Ho! Out of the Wilderness

"And the God of all grace, who called you to his eternal glory in Christ, after you have suffered a little while will himself restore you and make you strong, firm and steadfast." 1Peter 5: 11

Sometimes the sound of silence is deafening. Three years after the coma, surgery, and chemotherapy, Brenda's husband died with complications from a bone marrow transplant. He was 55 years old.

 She says: Having returned from the Houston hospital, I walked in my front door in my home in Ft Worth. Blinking my eyes, I could understand something clearly at last. The fragments and dust filtered slowly downward in the sunshine of the den of my home. I could almost feel the energy molecules jangling in the air. In the room, however, there was total and absolute lonely silence. Total and lonely silence wrapped around me. Silence like I had never known.

179

In our life journey, it may seem that God is silent.

But God is never silent. What looks like silence and inactivity to us is God allowing us the opportunity to listen to "the still small voice" and to see the provisions that He has made for us by faith. In Mark 10:30, it says that God is involved in every area of a believer's life--the very hairs on our heads are numbered. However, there are times when we must walk in obedience to the light that God has given us before He sheds more light on our path.

God speaks to us through His Word.

"For my thoughts are not your thoughts, neither are your ways my ways, says the Lord. For as the heavens are higher than the earth, so are my ways higher than your ways, and my thoughts than your thoughts. For as the rain comes down, and the snow from heaven, and returns not, but waters the earth, and makes it bring forth and bud, that it may give seed to the sower, and bread to the eater: So shall my word be that goes forth out of my mouth: it shall not return unto me void, but it shall accomplish that which I please, and it shall prosper in the thing where I sent it" (Isaiah 55:8-11).

Listening is tough. It reminds Brenda of her infant sons. In those days, we fed babies from baby food jars. The moment my eldest son Derek heard the pop of unscrewing the top of a baby food jar—coincidentally, this was a baby who had been happy only moments before--he would now burst into tears. With his eyes tightly shut and little mouth scrunched into a yowl, he suddenly remembered that he was hungry and wanted it NOW.

He was so busy complaining of a suddenly realized hunger, he couldn't see the food being delivered on a shiny baby spoon.

It reminds us that we get so busy with eyes shut and face scrunched in a yowl, we often don't see how the Lord is preparing our table with good food/blessings for us. We are so busy complaining; we can't see the something good that is coming. Prayers often reflect this.

And somehow, we come out of the wilderness. As we look at ourselves, we are in a moment between our past and our future. Just in case you keep trying and feel like you are getting nowhere with your face scrunched in a yowl, here is a thought. Your full blossoming could be in the invisible developing stage. It may be just before the fruit of your work can burst into bloom. Or it may be like Mary Magdalene just before the glorious sunrise!

Remember how we often stop inches before our victory?

Louis Pasteur was only a mediocre pupil in undergraduate studies and ranked 15th out of 22 students in chemistry. In 1872, Pierre Pachet, Professor of Physiology at Toulouse, wrote that "Louis Pasteur's theory of germs is ridiculous fiction." Pasteurization today has saved many lives.

27 publishers rejected Dr. Seuss's first book, "To Think That I Saw it on Mulberry Street". The 28th publisher got it right.

Decca Records turned down a recording contract with the Beatles with the evaluation, "We don't like their sound. Groups of guitars are on their way out." After Decca rejected the Beatles, Columbia records followed suit with a rejection.

When Pablo Casals reached 95, a young reporter asked him "Mr. Casals, you are 95 and the greatest cellist that ever lived. Why do you still practice six hours a day?" Mr. Casals answered, "Because I think I'm making progress."

As Michelle Obama, former First Lady, states in her book, Becoming: "I grew up with a disabled dad in a too-small house with not much money in a starting-to-fail neighborhood, and I also grew up surrounded by love and music in a diverse city in a country where an education can take you far. I had nothing or I had everything. It depends on which way you want to tell it." Later in the book, she goes on to say, "For me, becoming isn't about arriving somewhere or achieving a certain aim. I see it instead as forward motion, a means of evolving, a way to reach continuously toward a better self. The journey doesn't end."

And finally, in her first book, The Magnolia Story, Joanna Gaines who achieved one of television's top rated television programs said, "Life is never predictable. Life is never really manageable. If your mind-set is always, "I'm just surviving" it seems to me that would wind up being your mind-set for the rest of your life. You'd just get stuck in it. As a parent, as a wife, as a business owner, I simply decided "I'm not going to survive anymore. I'm going to thrive. . . I just realized that I had a choice to make every moment, on every day, with every decision."

Not a survivor, but a thriver. Suffering can produce perseverance as shown by these famous persons. Perhaps God is waiting for us to develop the maturity to appreciate the opportunities that we have.

OK, so here it is. Here are three ways to give some clarity and find the light in the wilderness.

First. Yes, we know how to pray. So, let's examine your prayers. Are they "God help me, "and "thank you" just as you drop off to sleep? Are they formal prayers with impressive words that sound good but ring hollow? Are they the same repetition but no thinking?

Why not try this? Make it an informal dialogue with a good and caring friend who knows your heart and listens to your heart-felt statements. The first step is to talk it over with Him as informally as you would with a friend. Eileen admits to having repetitive prayers for friends and family that sometimes she falls asleep before she gets to the end. The surprise to her is that when she gets up to go to the bathroom, she goes right into where she left off. She finds this strange but true. Brenda admits to being in a rut with her prayers.

Secondly, are you comparing the advice that earthly friends are giving you with the words of the Bible? For Brenda, the Psalms echo her thoughts and give solace. She loves to just open the Bible and every time something will leap out to her that she had overlooked.

Thirdly, research has proven that writing down our thoughts will often hasten our healing. As former English teachers, Eileen and Brenda loved seeing this healing effect on students. Many of you have started writing entries in a journal to help you get out of the Wilderness. But Christine, an intern at Brenda's church takes it one step further.

 First, Christine writes down her "talk" (prayer) with the Lord. Next, she puts on her God-thinking hat. She re-reads the prayer aloud and this time she reads aloud from God's perspective. What would he say?

 She then writes an answer to her own prayer with the advice and perspective that she believes the Lord would write. Here is an example that she gave and that we might try:

Hello Lord. It is me. Again. I haven't been praying or talking with you because I thought you might be too busy for this little problem. I hate to bother you. I try to save for the big stuff; I just can't get past it. I've tried. Can you give me a little help here, Lord? I need some answers. Oh, and by the way, could you hurry up?

Does this prayer sound familiar? Now, put your God-hat on.
How do you think the Lord would answer?
Here is how we think that He would answer:

*You are my child. I am happy to talk with you anytime. I want
you to come to me with big and small problems. I hear you.
Nothing can separate me from you. Remember to drop in and
talk with me every day. Or many times in the day. I love
hearing from you.*

*By the way, you have won the lottery! Not the scratch off kind,
but the unbelievable prize called life. What are you going to
do with your winnings? I'm hoping that you find the courage
to invest in your dreams and believe in yourself. I have sent
the Holy Spirit to help you find the truth. Read my Word. It
tells you of my promises. I do not forget promises. I am a
faithful God. There is so much more I want to say but my most
important message is that I love you. Everything will work out.
. . in my time.*

Sigh! By putting on your God-hat, it gives insight either at that
time or when you return to read the entry. You are now
looking from a different perspective. Try it! Journaling can
give you new insight. Later you may have the realization that
you have answered prayers you may have overlooked.

Then putting on your God-hat reminds you of that still small
voice within you. Comfort or answers will come!

 On the radio, Brenda heard a contemporary song that repeats
the Psalms. "Pain comes in the night, but Joy comes in the
morning." Joy comes with the dawning of light or recognition
that maybe this wilderness that you are going through is to give
some discipline to your purpose. Maybe it takes a thousand
sleepless nights to finally listen. Maybe the proof is in the
pudding.

Let's Discuss:

1. We have discussed three ways to help come out of the wilderness. The first is to have informal talks with the Lord (prayer). Have you treated the Lord as a caring friend who listens or delivered formal prayers that ring hollow? Are your prayers complaints?

2. The second is to check your perspective. Are you listening to friends' advice and checking it with God's Word? Have you tried reading a chapter of Psalms each night?

3. The third is to write down your talk (prayer). Then put on your God Hat and answer it as a loving and caring God would answer this prayer. Did it give you a higher and better perspective? As a loving parent, He might not answer the way we thought or in our human timeline.

4. Have you looked back at some prayers you made and thanked God because He did not give you what you asked for? Garth Brooks wrote a song called "Unanswered Prayers." His lyrics were "Sometimes when you're talking to the Man Upstairs" …Some of God's greatest gifts are the unanswered prayers." He said he wrote it after attending a football game with his wife and seeing his high school flame.

   In high school he had prayed every day for that relationship. Evidently the answer was "no." He looked at his wife and recognized the wisdom in the road he had traveled. He saw the wife he now had and his former unanswered prayers (so he thought) with perhaps the wrong person.

5. Think of something that you don't like about yourself. Keep that thought.

Brenda heard about a missionary from Ireland. Every day as a child in Ireland, she had prayed that God would change her brown eyes to blue. After all, most children around her in Ireland had blue eyes. Somehow, God left her young self with brown eyes.

Then, as an adult, she became a missionary in India. She realized that if she had blue eyes, it would have differentiated her from those she was serving in her life as a missionary in India. She wouldn't have fit in, where it really counted.

Now, think about what you do not like about yourself, especially as a child. Examine that thought. Is it something that God may have used in your adult life to a greater capacity?

Chapter Twenty: Hashtag Friendship

"Sometimes God makes two women friends, because if they were sisters, their mom couldn't have handled it."
(Anonymous.)

Thankfully, God does not expect us to journey alone in life. We need Community/Friends to support us. In our discussion of a life development plan based on the model of Jesus, we now enter the Third stage.

When Jesus left the **Wilderness** to pursue his **Purpose**, he recognized the importance of **Community**/Friends and immediately selected his twelve disciples. He came to live among men, and to associate closely with a few men as he began his ministry. He was a young rabbi, fresh from testing in the wilderness coming to the Sea of Galilee. He selected twelve men. Their relationship with Christ transformed them. It was not a one-way street. In times of trouble, Jesus wanted them with Him. In the garden he said, "Stay here and watch with me." In times of good news, when He was resurrected, in Matthew 28:7, He said," Go and tell my brethren to go to

Galilee and there they will see me." They were the first He turned to.

This relational experience of community is very important. The Bible is a love story. God wants and places a high priority on that love relationship with His people. Notice that Jesus made a simple call to the men. He gave the opportunity for a relationship with God by simply saying (in Mark), "Follow Me." He did not say, "Follow these rules and you may qualify." Being a sinner did not disqualify them. Most of the persons in the Bible were not stellar. Some were scoundrels. This does not disqualify us from having a relationship with Christ. The invitation is not a bunch of rules, but a simple invitation to "Follow." God knows the value of Community and relationships.

From Brenda: My field of expertise is Organizational Behavior. In my speaking presentations both in corporate America and even in China, I have emphasized the importance of collaboration. Collaboration (communicating a common goal) is the most effective way to gain productive teams in the workplace. A good manager will encourage collaboration. There are benefits. Collaboration promotes feelings of _importance_, usefulness, pride and self-respect in the workplace. In turn, the team can reach clearly established goals through optimism, and respect by the team leader.

This same principle does not only apply to corporate teams. It can be carried over to an individual.

Obviously, technology has produced tremendous communication from Instagrams, Facebook, and smart phones. We are more connected via technology than ever before. However, research studies are showing that Americans are twice as lonely as twenty years ago due to lessening face-to-face contact. It is said that the average teenager spends 8-9 hours daily in cyberspace. Yet this ability to connect seems to magnify the lack of ability to connect face-to-face.

Have you attended a sports event lately for your child? Look around. All the parents in the stands are glued to their emails, texting, etc. Look around again. It is the same story at a deli, riding public transportation, walking down the street or even one of the pinnacles of social activity--the manicure salon. Heads are down, checking messages at every spare moment.

Research further says whether in the workplace or home, the cause of many problems is mediocre quality or non- existing friendship.

Let us examine that statement. Whether the problem is divorce, obesity or being fired from a job, research finds the cause of dissatisfaction and the resulting problem of divorce, obesity or being fired is often that the person felt unloved or outcast. They did not feel part of a community. They did not find friendship to support them. This resulted in loneliness and dissatisfaction. This is especially true among women.

Therefore, the importance of friendship provides a new twist to gathering around the campfire in the days of old. Long ago we huddled to trade information for survival. In today's technology boosted world, the built-in need to connect has only magnified. We have an overload of survival information, but less connection. We need connection!

Jesus came out of the wilderness and carefully selected a community which we have named as the third step and an integral part of our self-development model. This need for friendship is now documented in the field of psychology. Research that is gaining more attention concerns the role of friends in our lives. Most of the past research on friendship has been with children and adolescents. More recently researchers are seriously addressing adult friendships in our lifespan. Author Carlin Flora's book, <u>Friendfluence</u>, explores the research on friendship. Flora made up the word "friendfluence," which is "the powerful and often unappreciated role that friends—past and present—play in determining our sense of self and the direction of our lives."

If you think about it, your environment and family have influenced your formative years. Once reaching adulthood, it is often personal friends who continually shape who you are today. Sometimes you are even the product of friends who are no longer your friends. You may still be reacting to something a friend long ago said to you. The friend is gone, but you are still reacting.

It is important to put energy and attention into finding and cultivating a close circle of friends. It also proves to be a health benefit. Studies show that senior citizens who live alone show signs of losing the desire to live without having someone to share ideas with. Once they move into a facility, with others of versatile and energetic mentality, they begin to look forward to the next day instead of dreading it. Research says that socialization contributes to energy gain and a lift to depression.

According to research by Flora, the perks of friendship include sharpening your mind, making you generally happier, knowing yourself better, becoming inspired to reach your goals, advancing your career, helping you meet romantic partners, and living a longer and healthier life.

Another research study says that having a Girl's Night Out where laughter abounds should happen weekly for good health. This sounds like being truly alive. Former First Lady Michelle Obama says in her book, <u>Becoming</u>, that this was important to her. "In elementary school, I usually marched home with four or five other girls in tow for lunch each day. "This began a habit that has sustained me for life, keeping a close and high-spirited council of girlfriends—a safe harbor of female wisdom."

Sometimes it is this safe harbor of friendship that helps you get through the life stages and change. Sometimes we are the sandwich generation: we have problems of children and problems with parents. An email from Eileen to Brenda is an excellent example. It reminds us of the saying: "A loyal friend laughs at your jokes when they're not so good and sympathizes with your problems when they're not so bad." Here is the email:

Greetings!
You have been in our thoughts even if you weren't in our emails! It has been rough around here. Joe's Dad had a stroke. Once he was stable, he was transferred to Connecticut for re-hab so Joe can visit and oversee his care. I hadn't counted on finding out that Dad at 80 had a "girlfriend" thirty years his junior. I should have trusted my gut when I met her earlier and thought to myself that she was not what he thinks.

He's smitten and wants them to move in together. (Even his long-time neighbors have questioned her motives). This little lotus blossom perseveres. Husband Joe is stuck in the middle.

Then, just for added interest, I got an eye infection, bronchitis and my asthma went nuts. It's been miserable. Sure hope you have a better story to tell! Send word on what you've been up to and plan to do next.
Much love Eileen and co

Other times, it is feedback/support from a friend that gets you through a tough time. Eileen gives another example of humor in humiliation. Eileen says: A while back, I bought a necklace in Egypt. Joe had been making business trips there and I tagged along on a few of the trips to Egypt. On my first trip there, I was scheduled to go on a tour, but it was delayed. I wandered around the hotel grounds until the time to meet in the lobby.

My well-honed shopping instincts led me to the Gift Shop. They were selling necklaces in every color of the rainbow. There was a scarab in the center and four gold-colored beads which separated chunky square blocks of stone with carvings. And one of them was the exact shade of turquoise as my outfit for that evening- a reception for the General who commanded the Egyptian military and his wife.

 Perfect – I'd show my appreciation for local crafts and make a fashion statement at the same time. Besides, they weren't expensive!

 I bought a dozen or so, thinking they'd make good gifts for folks at home.

That night there was a receiving line in the penthouse of the Military Attaché. Joe and I stood at the end, waiting for the honored guests to go through. As they approached, I caught the eye of the General's wife and saw the shocked expression on her face.

I really made an impression! She gave an elbow to her husband and nodded in my direction. As he looked over, his face morphed from smiling to incredulous. Then, it was our turn. I gave it my best smile and shook their extended hands. They were still looking at the necklace.

Score one for me! Only, they weren't smiling. They were looking at the necklace – and me- like they wanted to run.

I managed to find the wife of the attaché. I considered her a friend who would tell me the truth. I was puzzled.

I asked her about the necklace – which, I noticed, she was looking at strangely. Reluctantly, she explained that these "trinkets" were bought for children to play dress up games in.

I was wearing Barbie jewelry. With panache. In public. In full view of one of the most powerful men in Egypt. Go, girl.

I still have some of those necklaces. After all, they're pretty and not many folks know I'm wearing Barbie jewelry... unless I tell them.

Which I often do.

The way I see it, when you're very impressed with yourself, that's the time to grab a little humility. I do it in Barbie jewelry. (And it goes with so many outfits!) But I'm thankful for a friend who told me the humorous but humiliating truth.

Let's Discuss:

1. Helen Keller said, "Walking with a friend in the dark is better than walking alone in the light." Sometimes it is only with the help of a friend that you can get through the

transitions life throws at you. Can you name how certain friends have influenced you?

2. Has a friend helped you find humor in humiliation?

3. What do you think of Michelle Obama's habit of keeping a close and high-spirited council of girlfriends? Has it been a safe harbor of female wisdom for you? What did it look like in your life? Do you have a girl's night out that only has laughter.

4, Are you ready to take a deeper dive into a relationship with Christ? Statistical research shows Americans value the Bible . . .but most seldom read it consistently.

They settle for their understanding to be preached by priest or pastor. As an adult, are you basing your understanding of the Bible on answers provided by teachers when you were a child?

Are you willing to take God up on the privilege of relationship? It is possible to have a friend that never leaves you.

Chapter Twenty-one: Your Community—Drainers or Propellers

"Oil and perfume make the heart glad, and the sweetness of a friend comes from his earnest counsel." Proverbs 27:9

Sometimes our friend is a perfect stranger adding an obstacle or a stranger smoothing our journey. Eileen has an example of a life stage that can be overwhelming. "Community" assists with this problem.

Eileen states: The feeling that you have too much to do, and not enough time isn't unique, but it seems to happen more to young mothers. There is always something waiting in the wings—a "must do," followed by another and another. It is called Overload.

We were assigned to West Point when I was pregnant with our second child. When summer came, we planned to go to Breezy Point, New York for a week's stay with Joe's parents. Joe had spent every summer there from the time he was ten years old. The plan was to drive down with Brigid, our daughter and Eustis, our dog. To extend this time of leisure, I would leave early, and Joe would join us when getting off from work. Perfect logistics. But first...

- A stop at the commissary and PX for some things needed for the trip.
- An appointment for a booster shot for Brigid at the post clinic.
- A craft item for the auction at the Officers' Wives Club to drop off.
- To do a quick wash for Brigid's snuggle up items for bedtime. (A nightmare if I didn't have them and I couldn't bring anything less than immaculately sanitized to my mother-in-law's home.)
- A snack early for Brigid so she wouldn't get car sick.
- The car to load and the dog to empty.

OK. Seat belts in place, the door locked, and we were off.

Right before the toll on the New York Expressway, I called back to Brigid, who had been napping, to ask if Eustis were being a good dog. She said, "Eustis isn't here, Mommy. You left him at home." Now this was long before the time of cell phones. I was too far from home to turn around. I had to tell Joe that we had a problem. How? The friendly toll collector came to the rescue. I was clearly upset and very pregnant as I asked for the closest phone. She offered to call Joe and tell him the story. What a wonderful lady!!

Joe strapped Eustis, a large dog who was half collie and half shepherd into the front seat of his two-seater and started the drive to Breezy. When he got to the toll, he got some strange looks, but when he asked the man to pass his thanks on to the lady who made the call, this man was all smiles. He'd heard the story earlier of the pregnant woman who'd forgotten her dog. This large dog in a seat belt was an even funnier addition to the story.

I'll always be grateful to that kind lady. Thank God there are people like her to take the extra step when things seem in overload and just one straw too many for a person to handle. God often sends us help when we need it. Sometimes it isn't what we had in mind, but it's there.

A community provides valuable support to each other in life's circumstances. We get valuable insight and problem solving from a diversity of friends who have experienced similar life events (life stages such as pregnancy, parent of teenagers, divorce, etc.). The community of friend(s) understands because they have been there. Because these diverse friends know our situation so well, they can see things that we can't. What's the potential for your life if you really examined your friendships?

From Brenda: When I conduct executive coaching, I often ask executives to examine the people around them. They can be classified into three groups.

We surround ourselves with drainers, maintainers, and *propellers*. The **drainers** are the people who may love us dearly but hold us back with fear ("don't take that risk," "what would people think," "that cake (referring to a situation) is baked, don't mess with it." Or this may be a friend who texts, emails, or calls while whining and complaining. The whining (and drain) is as predictable as game replay. When you hear their voice, you brace yourself for the onslaught of negativity.

Maintainers are average. They see life as average, and for sure, they will not make a wave. They won't tell you the truth because it might be uncomfortable.

What we need in our community of friendship are the Barnabas, **the propellers**, the encouragers. For Paul, who had persecuted Christians, it was the trust and encouragement of Barnabas who introduced Paul to Christians who began to listen and not fear Paul. We need Encouragers. They are trusted truth tellers who help us when our perspective is incomplete or inaccurate. ("Your marriage could use some counseling with that problem," "Your finances are out of control"," Maybe you're not working on the right priority," "Maybe this is out of my pay grade, and you need professional help").

We take information/feedback from these Propellers because we know they have our best interest at heart. They correct us, hold us accountable and challenge us to grow beyond what is comfortable because they believe we can do it and they care. They help us to understand who we are without kidding ourselves and recognize what our perception of the world is.

On the other hand, we must recognize the drainers. When a coworker is yelling at you, a husband, child, or lover is berating you, and you realize you are being treated badly but unjustly, we need the strength to walk away. We can separate our own needs and desires from the drainers.

We can pay attention to that deep small voice inside us that wants to protect and take care of us. We have the option to feel safe and establish a boundary that is not to be bullied. There goes the grape jelly!

If you surround yourself only with maintainers, or drainers, there is no one who will challenge you to stop _____ (fill in the blank)

If you only follow your own instincts, or only rely on the kind words and prayers of maintainers, would you really find the truth of the matter? Have you given yourself permission to spend time only with those people you enjoy? Are you setting healthy boundaries between yourself and drainers?

From Brenda: I thought of myself as a supermom, juggling work and social volunteerism, while keeping a grateful heart towards my sons and husband. Or so I thought.

I talked to a friend about how a particular son in Middle School could achieve more (naturally I thought he was wonderful but could do so much more!). She took a deep breath and said, "Brenda, I don't know if I could live up to the bar you've set. You push yourself and expect others to push themselves just as hard. That's hard for a kid. It would be hard for me, even, as an adult." Poof! Maybe, just maybe, I was part of the problem. I needed this change of perspective.

I was creating a little person who was finding it was impossible to live up to high expectations. That bar was not enticing. It's difficult to hear the truth from a Propeller friend, but without it, we can't go where God knows we can go.

199

The propeller or truth teller might be whom God sends to help, challenge and inspire us to grow into the person He is calling us to be. Often Jesus was surrounded by drainers and maintainers who loved him but could not yet grasp his purpose. Peter, for example, didn't want Jesus to go into Jerusalem. He didn't understand what Jesus knew was His purpose.

From Eileen: Little children seem very wise at times. Unfortunately, the wisdom seems to evaporate by the time they are teenagers. Remember when I told you about the comment from my son that changed my attitude? When Brett was four, he looked up and he said, "You're not listening to me." I huffed back that I most certainly was listening. He said, "You're not listening with your eyes." Very true.

I've been trying to listen with my eyes ever since. It's not always easy, especially with an aging parent, an unruly teenager, a bigoted adult, a depressing friend.

My Mom's favorite cousin, Bill, was killed in the invasion of Anzio during World War II. His fiancée, Vera, stopped living that day. Her world became a bleak place with nothing inside but dark thoughts, complaints, and criticism. Mom asked me to keep up with Vera if Mom died first. Calling Vera was an ordeal.

Once I caught myself gently banging my head against the wall next to the phone. If I had a certain expression on my face, my husband would say, "Have you been talking to Vera?" She died at the age of 88, but she really died long before that. I never managed to break through her barrier of despair – not with happy news, family pictures, stories of long ago. Her Truth was that life wasn't fair and that she had been cheated by

God. She never changed.

When Brenda was traveling for her consulting work, a fringe benefit was her visits to our farm. She was here for our Grand-daughter's Baptism, for the town wide "Tractor Parade", for adventures to Hyde Park and to see the amazing fall foliage along the Hudson River. On one of her visits, she told me about a new man in her life. I was pleased for her. David's death was difficult. She looked happy again.

But then, little bits of her conversation started to disturb me. This man had relatives only a short drive away from us. They had visited these people, but he didn't want to come to see us. He was pressuring Brenda to make a permanent commitment – to marry him soon. I was thinking "too soon", but I mouthed platitudes about taking your time. The next thing I knew, they were married. Still, I was happy for her and hoped this was her answer going into the future. It wasn't.

Should I have been more forthright about my concerns? Would it have made a difference? Might it have ended our friendship? We'll never know. But what I do know is that not listening to that little voice in your head – or your heart – is always a mistake.

Hasn't it happened to you? I'm not advocating spurting out everything that enters your mind – just registering that there might be a cause for concern there. Remember – and listen with your eyes and your heart if you want to give truth to a good friend.

The friends you surround yourself with have a definite influence on your success.

The secret to your future may be hidden in your daily routine and your relationships. Old habits, comfortable old friends (relationships) and the stories (Lucy)we tell ourselves may be what is holding us back.

We may have to have some intentional faith building to renew our heart.

What do you think?

1, Have you examined your listening to friends or family? Is it with your eyes and your heart?

2.When is the last time you invited someone to tell you the truth? Did you hear with a grateful heart? Remember the Bible verse we started this chapter with: *"Oil and perfume make the heart glad, and the sweetness of a friend comes from his earnest counsel." Proverbs 27:9*

3. Can you identify the Drainers, Maintainers and Propellers in your life?

4. A Chinese proverb says, "Shared joy is double joy, and shared sorrow is half-sorrow." Have you experienced this double joy or half sorrow with friends?

5.Sometimes friends try to tell us something. We think we are the best assessor of what we do. If more than one person is telling us we have a problem, we have a problem. Do we make excuses?
Plutarch said, "I do not need a friend who changes when I change and who nods when I nod; my shadow does that much better." Do you agree and why?

Chapter Twenty-two: A grateful heart

"Let your roots grow down into him, and let your lives be built on him. Then your faith will grow strong in the truth you were taught, and you will overflow with thankfulness."
Colossians 2:7

What gets in the way of many of our friendships and even in our relationship with the Lord? What stalls or places obstacles in finding our Purpose? Eileen and Brenda think it is taking for granted the gift of friendship or relationships. Robert Louis Stevenson has said, "A friend is a gift that we give ourselves." Relationships are often the key to finding our Purpose. Relationships in our community must be laced with gratitude.

Unfortunately, too often in a long-term relationship, the appreciation of simple acts of kindness is replaced by taking kindness for granted.

A grateful heart goes by the wayside and the relationship is no longer seen as a gift. Sometimes resentment and criticism occur because the small kindnesses are no longer seen as a gift but an obligation. It can happen in a marriage or in a friendship.

From Eileen: I was recently struck by how important it is for a parent to teach their children to have a grateful heart. When Hurricane Sandy struck the East Coast, my daughter and her husband left Connecticut to go to Staten Island where her friends were affected by the storm.

She planned to take her 6-year-old with her. I volunteered to babysit fearing the situation might be too intense for a young child. My daughter said, "No, because I want Flynn to see despite the destructive power of the storm; friends can help friends."

Upon their arrival, the children of residents were given a safe place to play. One little girl asked in a quiet voice for socks because she had been evacuated in the night. Now she only had a nightgown and wet slippers. At some point the children were given baggies with snacks. Flynn brought her baggie to her mom and said she wasn't hungry now and would bring it later. My daughter replied that the children she was playing with had no food or clothing, thinking that Flynn would appreciate the gift of food. It was a teaching moment. Flynn's tearful response went deeper. She said, "You mean they don't even have their stuffed animals?" Somehow not having that security blanket (in her case Mr. Ruffles) and lack of safety surpassed the need for food or clothing. She was grateful for her own home, bed, and Mr. Ruffles that we all take for granted. It was the dawn of understanding of a grateful heart.

Not only accepting a friend as a gift but accepting gifts from friends is hard.

Eileen has this example. I was the eldest granddaughter and the first to marry. When Grandma died and Grandpa decided to move in with his eldest daughter, I was given Grandma's crystal and her nativity scene for Christmas. I have treasured these items ever since. The crystal was a wedding gift to her from her older sister, so I estimated it to be around one hundred twenty-five years old. Like Grandma, it held pride of place in my many dining rooms, and, like Grandma, it was used on every holiday and important occasion. Our many moves were hard on Grandma's crystal. Casualties came with each move.

My family knew enough to leave me alone when this unpacking was done. They also knew that we would be exploring every antique store for miles around in search of replacements for the fallen. Only twice did I have success.

When we moved to California to study Italian at the Defense Language Institute, we were able to visit with old friends who were stationed at the Presidio of San Francisco. On one visit for "the girls", my daughter and I stopped at an open-air flea market on the return drive. My daughter spotted antique glasses as we walked and, in an enthusiastic voice called out, "Oh, Mommy, it's Grandma's crystal!" The price went up on the spot, but I paid it gladly.

Time marched on – and casualties continued. Our move to Connecticut was particularly hard on Grandma's crystal. I mentioned it to a colleague at work, not knowing that her mother had owned an antique store. I drove home with her one afternoon to see the shop she was in the process of selling. Once again, I was drawn to the back wall where Grandma's crystal sat proudly on glass shelves. It was almost a complete set – far more than I had to start. I was thrilled and asked how much she wanted for the set. She refused to take any money and began to wrap the pieces on the spot. I kept insisting that she accept something, and she kept refusing. I brought the glasses home feeling guilty but elated.

The next day, I went to speak with my friend and to thank her again for the crystal – and to offer her payment once again. She smiled and told me that during the previous night she was wakened from a sound sleep by a loud crash. When she went to investigate, she found that all the glass shelves on the back wall had fallen, creating a domino effect, breaking everything on them. But, by then, Grandma's crystal was safe and sound in its new home. "So, you see," she said, "your grandmother was making sure that the crystal would be passed on for a long time to come."

Sometimes it's hard to accept a gift, especially a lavish one. That day I learned how to say, "Thank you" and let the giver have the pleasure of giving. My friend died last year. Each time I pass the China Closet, I now think not only of my beloved Grandmother, but also of a dear friend. Thanks, Debbie.

From Brenda: Ouch. This has been a hard one for me. Accepting a gift with graciousness is a lesson that I seem to have to learn again and again. I remember when I was a young schoolteacher just out of college with a minimal budget. I had a long winter coat. Fashion changed from long hemlines to knee hugging lengths. I wanted to cut off a huge hem to make my coat more fashionable. My grandmother who was an excellent seamstress volunteered to do this cumbersome hem for me. I surely could not have done it.

I tried on the coat, and it was truly a "much better" look. 'I was so pleased with the results that I grabbed my purse and handed cash over to my grandmother who was also on a tiny budget. She deferred.

In my haste to appear self-sufficient, worldly, and let's admit it, pride that I now had cash, I pushed the cash into her hands. I thought I was being generous, knowing she had very limited means. Later, she quietly told my mother how much it had meant to her to have the opportunity to do a labor of love for me. She couldn't really afford expensive gifts, so she had been happy to do this for me.

My mother sadly shook her head and said, "Brenda, you took away her gift. You must learn to accept gifts with a simple thank you."

Since that time, I have tried to recognize what a gift may cost in terms of effort and intention as well as value. While in college, I had returned a necklace gift from my younger sister because it was a duplicate of something I had already. Thirty years later I found out that she was still hurt because I had not recognized how she had shopped and selected carefully for that gift. She had shopped with her heart. To her it seemed careless or heartless of me while I had only thought it was a practical move not to have a duplicate necklace.

Currently, I try never to go through a door that has been opened for me without smiling a thank you. How often have you held open a door for someone and they passed through without acknowledging your presence?

I was really impressed with my daughter-in-law Ashley when she chastised her little daughter over not being properly polite after opening a Christmas present. She reminded my granddaughter in a gentle voice that they had recently talked on the importance of a grateful heart. My friend, Kay Custis, and I discussed how important a thank you note is and how this seems to be a dying custom. The older generation has let a thank you note slide into oblivion as a role model for the younger generation. I applaud that gentle voice of Ashley's to her children about the importance of a grateful heart.

A grateful heart is a tough one. I think it is a control issue. We are on a constant quest to say, "I got this!" "I can do it by myself." How often do we get in an elevator and re-punch the buttons that are already lit? We slowly smile at the others in the elevator, knowing that we have just re-done their perfectly good actions. Nobody wants to be controlled.

 The lack of refreshed gratitude suffocates a friendship, marriage or even a relationship with the Lord. The lack of control adds to our fear and the lack of gratitude keeps us from accomplishing our Purpose.
What do you think?

1. Have you learned to have a grateful heart and let the giver have the pleasure of giving? This is a tough one for self-sufficiency and pride. When has a friend helped you with this self-sufficiency and pride?

2. Eleanor Roosevelt said," Many friends will walk in and out of your life, but only a true friend leaves a footprint on your heart." Do you have a heartfelt friend that you need to acknowledge your gratefulness with a phone call, surprise text or handwritten note?

Chapter Twenty-three: A Bright Sadness

*'**Ri**se up, take courage and do it." Ezra 10:4*

What do you want to be when you grow up? Think back to the first time you were asked this question. Generally, we were five years old, trying to decide on a Halloween costume. But, as you grow up, you must come to a decision.

Life is transformation in our different life stages. We have arrived! We now enter the fourth stage of development which is finding our **Purpose**. In the last chapter we talked about

Community. We emphasized the importance of friendship, and the effect gratitude has on relationships.

Surprisingly, there is a link and a clue. It is based on science. The key to finding our **purpose** is neurologically linked in our brain to gratitude. Gratitude connects us to something larger than ourselves. Science is proving there is a mindset link of having gratitude to finding our Purpose.

Gratitude provides the emotional foundation to build our **purpose**. You start finding your purpose when you start counting your blessings.

If you are reading this book to get over your fears and discover your purpose, you probably feel driven to make a positive impact on the world. You want to make a difference.

Therefore, Berkeley psychologist Kendall Bronk notes that research has shown that children and adults who are able to count their blessings are much more likely to "contribute to the world beyond themselves."
In other words, if we can see how others make our world a better place, we'll be more motivated to give something back.

Altruism and gratitude are neurologically linked. They have the same reward circuits in the brain. Gratitude connects us to finding our purpose.

When moving toward our **Purpose**, it feels like the Texas two-step. It's one step forward and two steps back. Eileen told me that she and her granddaughter, Flynn, were approaching a wily horse in their fenced area in Connecticut. The horse was trying to outsmart them. Eileen was warned by her then 5-year-old granddaughter, "Nonna, you just have to walk with purpose."

From Brenda: Let's face it. Walking with purpose is both physical and mental. Once you think you have the hang of a life stage, life taps you on the shoulder. We move from one Life stage to another whether we like it or not. Last year I was sitting on the balcony of a classic log cabin in Telluride, Colorado. I had not sat and soaked in the mountain air from a cabin in too long a time. Life for me has changed from that energetic/frenetic all-male family to a new status. I am now a grandmother and a single woman.

What a change in perspective. Physically, if I just focused on the "now" of that balcony seat, there were definite contrasts. The fresh breeze in August in Colorado is much different from the 100 degrees heat I left behind in Dallas. It was simply wonderful to breathe in deeply – and oddly a bit unsettling.

Memories tinged each breath. My three energetic sons turned into fine men. They are now fathers. They have gifted me with four girls and two boys for grandchildren. Not only has my physical "location" changed in this moment from heat to mountain air, but also my position from mother (maker of the rules) to grandmother (with the hugs but don't overstep the new family lines).

Motherly advice, once given freely daily, now produces a thin line between laughter and pain of misunderstood intentions. Mom's advice may now be seen as "out of touch." Motherhood wasn't easy. It was the warmup act to grandmother and mother-in-law—a tad tougher where a careless word may cause hurt that is not intentional. That is why Richard Rohr in <u>Falling Upward</u> calls the second half of our life a "bright sadness." The second half brings bright sadness and sober happiness.

There is a changed capacity in this life stage. We now can hold life creatively with less time pressure or anxiety. Then again, the boon of less anxiety has a counter point. There is less respect for our "creative" way of problem solving. Our way of solving problems may be out of touch, old fashioned or out of bounds for younger loved ones.

Meridel Le Sueur wrote, "Survival is resistance." Since women have gained more independence, we have the freedom to throw off old definitions of what we "should" be doing at sixty or beyond. We resist outdated pictures of being elderly. We are energetic, capable, and intelligent. Even if we have been lifelong extroverts, we can enjoy solitude, but rebel at loneliness. However, there is a fine line between laughter and the pain of misunderstood intentions. My adult sons tell me I am doing something just like "Nanny." I know that is an insult. They considered my mother eccentric in her later life. I, on the other hand, am beginning to understand her. I, too, brush away tears after a particularly good family visit as my son's family drives away. They laugh; I have misty eyes.

I must perform self-nourishment, transform my attitude, and seek a deeper connection with meaningful people in my life. It is Redesign or decline.

By simply changing our position – mentally as well as physically in a life stage – we open our eyes and minds to see things differently. Sure – we all know this. I have friends in Texas, Florida, Colorado, Alabama, Connecticut, and Europe (you know who you are).

I visit them and try to imagine what my life would be like if I moved to a new physical location where my friends lead quite different lives. Yet, what I learned in this ah-ha moment on the outdoor balcony was that until I changed and transitioned mentally to my new position, as grandmother from mother, I didn't really *get it*.

Whether I wanted to or not, I had to change from mother to grandmother. Move over, Rover. The rules and acceptance of my advice are not the same. Unless asked, we must remain quiet. Grand mothering requires diplomacy on both sides.

This also is true of our mindset in this life stage; we must be *in it* to really see it. I did not get it with my parents—now I'm beginning to see what they felt. It is often a friend who is not afraid to tell us the truth that helps us *see* the truth. Sometimes it is that quiet voice from the Lord that helps us see. Redesign or decline. Bitter or better?

How often do we get into a rut of seeing things from the same point of view, perspective, and set of lenses based on where we are at the time?

What can we gain by shifting – even just a little – to see things from the other point of view? Eileen voluntarily does this as she thinks how to market her ceramics for the Women's Guild Sale. Eileen questions: What would happen if we stopped selling our product the way we want to sell and position what we are selling the way the buyer wants to buy? What would happen if we genuinely tried to put our feet in the other person's moccasins in a negotiation for selling? Do we need to look twice?

As Brenda travels, doing management behavior seminars, she constantly finds (whether in China, Russia, the U.S., or Europe) that people slip into a competitive win/lose perspective. They think that they win only if the other person loses. They think they must snuff out someone else's candle to make theirs burn brighter. She is constantly talking about win/win via collaboration. This is much better in conflict resolution than I win/you lose mindset.

The importance of collaboration is not lost among the younger millennials in the audience. Some of the older executives fold their arms with a frown over the newer perspective of collaboration and the gift of receiving feedback. She especially noticed this in China and Russia when she gave seminars where change is slowly taking place in the workplace for a more democratic lifestyle if indeed, it is at all.

Ironically as we mature, we no longer need to change or adjust other people to be happy. We don't have to play the "I win/you lose "game. Instead, it is, how do we make this "win/win?" Happy partner, happy life.

That is what makes the difference in seeking our purpose in a new, evolving life stage. Instead of confusion, we get clarity. We learn to let go of fearing the consequences but feel gratitude for the good benefits and look at our constantly changing circumstances.

This leads us back to friendship. What feedback can a good friend (whom we trust) give so we have a win/win perspective about life? Can a friend help us to let go of rash judgments, stop holding on to old hurts or feeling the need to punish other people? Or as a granddaughter, Skylar, pointed out, it is not so much to have what you love, but to love what you have. (How do they make granddaughters so smart?) I think she was quoting Taylor Swift's song.

Are the Millennials teaching the Boomers about gratitude?

This is the "bright sadness" that leads us into a mature life, no matter what our chronological age is, as we find our Purpose.

The rules are different now. Humorously, Brenda says, "When I was a child, I didn't want to sleep or nap, but I had to. As an adult, I sometimes wanted to sleep but I couldn't. Now, it seems sleep apnea has claimed me, and I don't want to sleep, but I fall asleep watching tv. Circumstances change.

Now I am learning to go ahead and use the good China plates or the crystal—what am I saving it for? Eileen learned this after her mother's death. Eileen found wonderful gifts that she had given her mother-- still in boxes. Her mother had saved these special gifts for "special occasions." She never got to enjoy them by always "saving." Eileen decided that she was going home and using all her "good stuff." Not using them was fruitless.

We don't have to climb the ladder. We need to look around and enjoy the view.

We must find new ways to stay engaged and empowered. When Brenda attended a high school reunion, they each congratulated themselves on getting to the stage in life where they weren't trying to "one up" each other, but simply enjoying the satisfaction of not hoarding, collecting, or trying to impress. Again, that is not a chronological maturity, because many Millennials have been telling this to Baby Boomers in the workplace.

We can simply enjoy the brightness in each other. It is only then that we can be open to finding our Purpose. It is only then that we have looked twice.

From Eileen: We don't always anticipate the changes that come in life. As Brenda said, we need to learn to adjust our life stage with open eyes and minds. When Joe got orders to go to Italy, we were scheduled for world famous language school in Monterey, California. On the first day we were asked to complete our language skills. With every imaginable language, you designated numerical value. Joe scanned the list since he had studied Latin in high school and college. Finally, he raised his hand and asked what number he should put for Latin. The answer was "Zero." That should have been a clue.

After so many years in aviation, Joe at the age of forty, had lost a considerable amount of his hearing in the extremely high and very low ranges. Now we realized his ability to hear this new language of Italian and reproduce the pronunciation was going to be a huge challenge. From morning to night, there was no room for goofing off. Every word was in Italian whether you understood or not. Our children were vested in the process and brought us milk and cookies at night, because they knew if Joe did not make a sufficiently high score on this college course equivalent, the trip to Rome was off. We really felt that we were "supposed" to accept this international challenge.

Many people are not comfortable in role playing. Yet this class required functional scenarios for communication (for example, hailing a taxi, opening a bank account). Joe was handed a card telling him that he had arrived in Rome's train station with a multitude of luggage and needed help to get to the hotel. Following the directions, he stood, cleared his throat and raised his hand to signal a bellboy. With command, he called "Finocchio.!"
There was a sharp intake of breath from our teacher. She turned to me and said, "Madam, that word is the Roman detrimental slang for a gay man. It has been our experience that such mistakes are often repeated. Please make sure YOU call the bell boy. The word is "Facchino." What's a vowel or consonant between friends?

When graduation day came, Joe got a standing ovation from the faculty and fellow students. Everyone knew how hard he had worked to make that day possible. I was very proud of him. He never gave up. He was great at reading and writing (Latin) but listening and speaking were nearly impossible for him.

Joe decided that when he was on the street, he wouldn't make that same mistake. If anyone stopped him on the street, they would probably just be asking directions, so he'd answer, "non son di qui" (I'm not from here). That worked beautifully until one day, a man approached him at the bus stop. He asked Joe a question in Italian. Joe gave the standard answer. The man replied in beautifully accented British English, "Sir it's the same time here in any language."

Putting yourself in a situation where you could look ridiculous, makes us withdraw.

Putting new information in our brain is exhausting and a challenge. It's not impossible if you're motivated. And sometimes if you're lucky, you get milk and cookies from a supportive family as you pursue what you believe is your Purpose and calling.

Let's Discuss:

1. A bright sadness is letting go and letting the consequences flow. Do you worry about having what you love or love what you have?

2. Sticking your neck out is rarely a comfortable position, but in taking a chance with something new and challenging, you can learn that you are capable of new and gratifying things. When was the last time you pushed yourself toward what you believe is your Purpose?

2.Connection to others and Community can help you reach your destination of Purpose.

 By seeing purpose in others, you are more likely to see that it is possible for you, too. Eileen's mother and aunt were discouraged from pursuing nursing careers by their parents. When her aunt was widowed at the age of 50, she decided to go to nursing school. Eileen's mother decided if her sister could do it, she could do it. Eileen's mother became a licensed practical nurse at the age of 55. Eileen had to change her wedding date because it conflicted with her mom's graduation. Are there some role models that you need to talk to, so you can discover if it is a possibility for you?

4. Do you experience gratitude daily? Do you count your blessings? This is a step toward finding your Purpose. Remember the turtle. He doesn't make progress unless he sticks his neck out.

Chapter Twenty-Four: Remember your First Love

An interesting part of finding your purpose is to remember your first love. When Eileen's husband Joe was in college, he was unsure of a major. So, he took several occupational preference tests from the college to find a major. He was a City Kid, growing up in Queens, New York. To his surprise and his parents' bewilderment, he tested strongly as a "farmer." Eileen can tell you more of the story.

"What are you going to be when you grow up?" That was the joke between my husband and I throughout his military career. It was followed by "And where do you think you'll live?" Assignment after assignment, we'd assess the location—was this the place we'd eventually settle? Some were a clear "no!" while others held possibilities. Each time we'd discuss retirement from the Army, Joe's final comment was always,

"As long as it's not in the northeast." Clearly, God had other plans.

When we moved back to the states from our Italian assignment, we requested St. Louis. It was a family joke that our version of "military assignments" and the rest of the Army's ideas were vastly different. My cousin once asked his mother if Joe were in the CIA. Clearly, the places we lived didn't scream "Army." St. Louis was one of them. Joe's work at AVSCOM-Aviation Systems Command- combined his aviation background and the logistician/supply chain specialist which he had become. We thought this last assignment would be in a familiar place, a community where housing was affordable and schools excellent. I could return to St. Louis University's English as a Foreign Language Program and teach with old colleagues and friends. There were jobs available for Joe following retirement and it would be the end of moving. Or so we thought.

Joe got a call from a General that he had worked for in Europe asking him to "stop by" for a chat the next time he was on the east coast. That chat led to a job offer from Sikorsky and –you guessed it—a move to the northeast. We found a small farm in Connecticut, complete with an attack ram and a "naughty" goat. As city slickers, we weren't familiar with "naughty" farm animals. We quickly learned that this goat was Houdini and would escape on a regular basis. Phone calls from strangers-who quickly became friends-told us that our goat, "Chloe" (the name was already given) was walking down Main Street.

The Guinea hens we bought to control the insect population were fascinated by our neighbor's new pick-up. They pecked the paint into polka dots. Try explaining that to your insurance company. The menagerie grew over the years. Lessons were learned. Our accountant explained that we'd never be able to take the "Farm Credit" because we'd never make a profit. Yet, it was "home", finally and completely home. And, thirty years later, Joe found a satisfying purpose of combining consulting in logistics but at home as a farmer. Today a portion of the farm has been placed as an animal rescue. So today, the dysfunctional and geriatric animals are still coming in, but now it is a legitimate and a long-cherished dream.

As Joe found out, circumstances change, and it may be a winding road to find your Purpose. The person you were yesterday might not be the person you are tomorrow. We can feel life falling apart as we place our dreams on hold. Career choices often take a back seat to obligations or expectations of others. Career shifts due to job loss, job restructuring or even promotions place dreams on hold. There is stress, drama, and distraction both in our personal and professional life in finding our Purpose.

Rethink, reinvent, regain. Our purpose gets buried beneath life's challenges in different life stages.

From Brenda: When motherhood was forefront, my "purpose" as a mother trumped almost everything else. Just as our nest was emptying and my motherhood demands were lessening, my husband contracted leukemia. The journey of his illness and death, however, was in some ways a partnership. We fought his illness, and it gave us purpose. We fought his leukemia together with every feasible option for three years. Then, following his death, the next year was a cocoon of grief and adjustment. That year brought a new purpose: being strong (appearing sane) for the sake of my sons and my career and adjusting to a deep loneliness and grief. This was followed exactly one year later by the sudden death of my mother due to a quick and fatal stroke.

I looked back over my roles and identities. I had changed jobs over the years in pursuit of career passion. My professional identity had been evolving. It was not always out of choice but necessity that my identity had changed. As the years passed, I found that I could do more international consulting, especially if I did some of it on a volunteer basis in mission trips. I volunteered during my vacations and taught management consulting at Russian American Christian University in Moscow, and the University of Guilen in China, etc. I have found my professional purpose by adding bits and pieces and experimenting. I am still reinventing. I am still learning how the Lord can use the talents He has given me. Rethink, reinvent, regain. Look twice. Redesign or decline.

Consequently, in finding your professional purpose, you will notice there are three mindsets in your career. I, personally, have experienced all three. There is the "paycheck" mindset. That means the job is not very satisfying, and you are just there to get a paycheck so you can follow your passion/purpose elsewhere. This is the "survive" mentality, not the "thrive" mentality.

Then there is the "career" mindset where advancement, salary, title, span of control is your strategy. Achievement is your purpose, and your focus is singular or inward. Everything else takes second place. I thought Vice President looked good on my resume following my husband's death.

Finally, there is the "purpose" mindset where you are involved, passionate and innovative in making a difference. You are committed to looking forward and your focus is outward rather than inward. Making a difference is your purpose.

I never knew going from caterpillar to butterfly could be so full of angst.

My professional purpose, of course, integrates with my personal purpose. So here I am--a combination of teen-age angst with a pimple propping up my wrinkles. Why am I still getting both pimples *and* wrinkles? We are full of contrasts!

My mindset is that of the Boomers who believe that the age of 60's is the new 40's. Do you think my Depends will get caught up in my thong underwear? My nipple ring caught sagging on my knees. Just kidding. Neither thong, nose ring nor Depends do I wear—however, my chest may no longer be perky. They call it the chest of drawers' disease. Your chest falls into your drawers. I'm working on that issue via my Dance/exercise classes at the gym!

I want to ensure my purpose and that my life has meaning in terms of giving. Winston Churchill said, "You make a living by what you get. You make a life by what you give." Traveling on overseas mission trips has become something I try never to say "no" to. Aligning myself with Christian Universities, I find this has been both a blessing to others and a blessing to me.
One summer in Canada, I participated in a Delta Gamma service project for the Canadian National Institute for the Blind. I saw true courage and joy in the face of a blind eight-year-old who paddled and splashed in a boat in the lake with no fear and no sight. It was I who gained a true appreciation for the courage of those with limited sight and the wonder of eyesight.

As we rethink and reinvent our purpose by shedding old fears, let us each do the extraordinary in ordinary circumstances. Let laughter well up from a deep and vital joy in the beauty that surrounds us if we only appreciate it. Let us be like Erma Bombeck who said, "When I stand before God, I would hope that I have not a single bit of talent left, because I used everything you gave me."

So that is where we are. How about you? What is holding you back? Have you experienced some old assumptions and fears that are keeping you from transitioning into a new life with purpose? Have you held back because of a need for perfection (the right time, no money, etc.) We all have moments of courage. Taking yourself into a new career that plays on your strengths and passion may be a small tweak or a large leap.

Sometimes we get caught in the trap of allowing others to make decisions about our purpose and our perseverance. Paul struggled with this also. In Philippians 3:13-14, he said, *"Brothers and Sisters, I do not consider myself yet to have taken hold of it. But one thing I do: Forgetting what is behind and straining toward what is ahead, I press on toward the goal to win the prize for which God has called me heavenward in Christ Jesus."*
Paul is saying to press forward to what God is pressing upon us. In these verses Paul says he has not yet taken hold of all God is calling him to do, but he is straining to press ahead. Paul is pressing for progress over perfection by growing and moving forward.

What about you?

1. Are old assumptions keeping you from new playgrounds and new purpose? Have you learned to look at beauty from the inside out so transition starts with the insides?

2. When you stand before God will you have used all your talents? What about a volunteer project you should consider?

Chapter Twenty-Five: Finding Purpose – Getting Woo-hoo !

Who is going to harm you if you are followers of that which is good? 1Peter 3:13

By now, you have noticed that Eileen and Brenda believe in attitude adjustment. We are getting specific now on finding your purpose after you have let your fears get behind you. Life is meant to be lived, not studied. A crucial step in finding your **Purpose** is to stop thinking and start doing.

You must step out on faith to find joy in a new life stage situation. Then persevere. A dream is a dream if it stays in your head. You must act on your belief to make it reality. Finding your **Purpose** is finding your passion. What is something that is so enjoyable to you that you feel energy because of it, not drained at the end of the day?

There are psychologically proper ways to phrase this idea. However, all of us want to know a burning question: How do you get woo-hoo in your life? How do you even pronounce woo-hoo? Go ahead, say it out loud. You can't have it if you don't say it.

Woo-hoo is different for different folks. *It* is the magic of "I can." If we wait until tomorrow to be happy, we miss the beauty of today. Woo-hoo is laughing aloud, feeling good!

Sometimes we get so used to feeling bad, we forget what it feels like to feel right.

From Brenda: I love it when I play with my grandchildren. We have "Gram" days. When they go down a slide at the playground, I encourage them to shout woohoo. We shout. My grandsons (David and Jackson) find this extremely easy to do. They slide; then jump up with joy to run do it again. Now Olivia must do the same tricks as her brother does. This works in the pool, too. A toddler or even three boys on the ski slope are not weighed down by "should" and "impossible".

I also get creative in my cooking. When my two granddaughters came for a sleepover, I found that they enjoy making pancakes with me. But what doesn't taste better if you add a few chocolate chips? So we sprinkle in chocolate chips with the pancake mix, to make "Gramcakes." Some of this is self-defense to make something that they like.

Through the years, I have cooked less and less. Milk gets out of date. My adult children immediately open my refrigerator and check for the dates on eggs, milk, salad dressing before they use it. It's amazing how quickly out of date things become in that refrigerator—I think it is a warped time machine.

Somehow, what I make and what the pictures in the magazines look like are not a match.   One time I was inspired to make pink deviled eggs for Easter. I thought that would be special and you only add beet juice to make it pink. The result? Not so much. It was **Not** Woo-Hoo. . . but Watch Out!

I think my sons have lost their sense of humor. They made excuses and voted for a "cook out" grilled on **their** patio for the next Easter. I know my mother had her poodles dipped in pink for Easter when they were groomed. At the time, I thought that was weird. I am beginning to understand. I used to ask my son if he wanted a grilled cheese sandwich. He would reply, "Who is making it, you or Dad?" That sounds insulting but the truth is that David grilled a beautiful grilled cheese-- I preferred to microwave the sandwich which doesn't exactly turn out the same woo-hoo.

When was the last time you experienced a woo-hoo—what was it? Here are some thoughts about steps to reaching woohoo.

First, how do we start experiencing woohoo? The future is not limited by what we can see right now. Part of speaking the language of woo-hoo is letting go and letting God. Think right now about what you'd like to see happen. What attributes do you want to gain? Places to visit? Things to happen this next year? Now think, what attitude or behavior is blocking that from happening? Can you let it go? Can you focus on your strengths not your weaknesses?

As parents, if your child brings home a report card of A, B, B, C and D. What do we immediately focus on?

The D.

Now, as adults, we have achieved competence. It is time to focus on the A. What do we enjoy and excel in? We need to lead with our strengths. Embrace the excellence.

A prayer request: God, help me to push myself to experience something new each week. Help me to start living my life with woo-hoo. Help me make the journey from fear and control to letting go and stepping with you into my true power. Help me to see the possibilities of my strengths and what I find energized and enjoyable.

Second, if we placed a two by four plank on the ground and walked its length without falling off, it'd be easy. Now place a couple of bricks on either end, raising it a few inches. It's a little harder. It's the same two by four plank. We can do it.

Now imagine placing the same two by four plank suspended the height of your house. Would you try it?

The higher the stakes, the harder it is to maintain our balance. That's what fear does in our life. Are you allowing a worst-case scenario to upset your balance? Put the situation back on the ground, removing the fear that your mind has created. This is rhetorical. I'm not suggesting that you run out and suspend a two by four plank to test your courage. I'm just asking if fear is making you continue to do things the same way. Then do you expect to get a different outcome?

After my husband David died, I have tried to do one new thing every week. Some are very small. Other things are bigger. One summer I knew I needed to change my golf grip. I wanted to get a little more distance, but I ended up hacking at the ball. My son Justin gently suggested that I take lessons. Hmmm. A little expert advice from a golf pro has given me more distance and control. I'm still not exactly good, and I think I've compromised to a half new grip somewhere in between. But I love to be outdoors. Oh, don't try shouting woo-hoo on the golf course when you get it right. It disturbs the men.

A prayer request: God, help me let go of unreasonable fears and impatience, the ones that are preventing me from living my life. Don't let me wait until tomorrow to be happy, so I miss out on the beauty of today. Help me to shake up my routine and my grip so I get a shift in perspective.

Naturally, Mother Theresa said it better. No, she didn't call it woo-hoo. She said we should allow our soul the freedom to sing, dance, praise, and love. There is an oft quoted prayer that is attributed to her:

May today there be peace within
May you trust God that you are exactly where you are meant to be.
May you not forget the infinite possibilities that are born of faith.
May you use those gifts that you have received, and pass on the love that has been given to you.
May you be confident knowing you are a child of God.
Let this presence settle into your bones, and allow your soul the freedom to sing, dance, praise and love.
It is there for each and every one of us.

From Eileen: I love this idea of woo-hoo, especially since Brenda and I have shared woohoo moments. Last summer we went on yet another adventure together. We saw this sign in a Chocolate shop.

"Life should not be a journey to the grave with the intention of arriving safely in a well-preserved body, but rather to skid in sideways, chocolate in one hand, body thoroughly worn out and screaming, "Woo-Hoo, what a ride!"

Finding your passion and Purpose may require sacrifices. You'll know it is right for you if you don't mind the sacrifice.

For Brenda: In order to get my Ph.D., I was working full time (tuition benefits!) for an aerospace company Monday-Thurs. On Fridays I was on the road at 5 AM to drive 3 hours to U.T. Austin. I attended class Friday and Saturday, arriving home at 4 PM on Saturday. It required my sweet husband's help in getting my sons to Friday and Saturday sports activities, but I honestly felt "alive" rather than tired. I was very grateful for the opportunity.

In Eileen's case, she and Joe took turns getting master's degrees with small children at home. Eileen was working, mothering, helping Joe, volunteering at church, serving on committees at the Officer wives club and going to the University program at night. Not surprisingly, she developed an ulcer halfway in the university program. The Doctor sternly looked at her and stated, "You must cut back. What do you plan to remove from your activities?" She thought he was crazy. What could she possibly remove?

 He gave her permission to say no. She re-examined her priorities and finished her master's by holding off on volunteerism. Cutting back is not making the parts of your life smaller but making the important parts of your life larger.

 How can you make the important parts of your time larger? Have you exercised the ability to say no so you can get to the yes that meets your personal needs?

How about you?

1. Are you willing to step out on an adventure and get some woo-hoo? Woo-hoo is the magic of "I can" "laugh out loud, feeling good" and recognizing our passion. In trying to find your Purpose, does your job or role in life make you feel connected, worthwhile and energized? Or do you feel drained?

Do you need a change in perspective? Are you leading with your strengths and passion? What deeply moves you? What are you drawn to? Make a list of these.

2. Are you ready each day for adventure? Try out some pathways via small or large activities to see if it gives you energy. What are you naturally good at? Make a list of your abilities.

3. Do you have recurrent dreams or ideas to give you clues about what your Purpose is? Some clues are this: when you need some energy or happiness, do you retreat to the kitchen, do you go outdoors, do you entertain small children by reading to them, do you write in a journal, or organize groups or projects, speak to audiences, etc. What gives you energy? Brenda found that although she really enjoyed researching, she felt drained at the end of the day. When she stood before an audience, she walked out energized. Make this list of happy places.

4. Are you ready to shake up your routine? Try a shift in your perspective. Is it your attitude? Change what you can change about your attitude that may be blocking your Purpose.

   a. Be aware there is a mind-attitude connection. Your actions will be influenced by your foremost thoughts of gratitude.

   b. Nourish your brain with empowering thoughts about yourself and others. Listen to upbeat music and talk to Encourager/Propeller friends that put you in a positive mood.

c. Get your heart pumping. Exercise. You'll feel more energetic if you move!! Aerobic dancing in exercise class is fun!

d. Write a list of small daily goals. When you accomplish one, celebrate the achievement by flexing your arm and saying, "yes!"

e. Again, add gratitude to your attitude.

5. It is not "what" you want to be when you grow up, but "all you can be." Learn to live with ambiguity. Is there a way to merge your talents into a job? There is not just one job out there for you. You have multi potential. Have you looked twice?

6. Now look for an intersection. Look twice at the lists you made above. Where does your Passion, your Talents, your Needs, and your understanding of what God would have you do make an intersection or overlap? What you "do" and what you're good at (talents) and finally when do you feel energized? Where is the overlap? How can you move from complacency to a calling where you have spent time talking it over with God?

Chapter Twenty-Six: Birds of Worry Landing on Your Head

Finding your purpose is a little like the Chinese proverb. "That the birds of worry and care fly above your head, that you cannot change. But that you allow them to nest in your hair, that you can change." You do have control over your decisions.

What if women paid attention to what they wanted and moved with confidence and joy toward their deepest desires? What if women felt a genuine empowerment from the True Source, a God who believes in your person because He knows and created you? As 2 Timothy 1:7 says, *"For God has not given us the spirit of fear, but of power, and of love, and of a sound mind."*

In the past, women have been socialized to measure success by the person they identify with. Often it was the person they helped to succeed that was called successful without their being in the spotlight or given credit for the accomplishments. It is a new day. We can step beyond our fears. We can find purpose in each changing life stage.

However, we cannot allow our Purpose to be defined by achievement- based measures. Instead, our Purpose is to be true to our heart and find what God would have us do and be.

Therefore, how we find our purpose is right there in the Bible. In Hebrews 5:12-14, *"In fact, though by this time you ought to be teachers, you (meaning we are being spiritually immature, sluggish and mentally lazy) need someone to teach you in the elementary truths of God's word all over again. You need milk, not solid food. . .But solid food is for the mature, who by constant use have trained themselves to distinguish good from evil."* The spiritually immature rarely focus on, or struggle with ethical and moral consequences of faith. The spiritually immature do not radiate Christianity. Other people can hardly tell that they are Christian either from their statements or behavior. Instead, their statements are hesitant, bashful, and sometimes vague.

Unfortunately, many of us are Sunday morning Christians getting fed without thinking or without applying it on Monday morning. Eileen says there is a slang expression among Catholics denoting the spiritually immature. They call them "A & P" Catholics. This stands for ashes and palms. They only attend services to get ashes and palms (Lent through Easter).

To become spiritually mature is to find God's purpose for our lives and to train ourselves via discipline of reading God's word to distinguish good from evil. Paul tells this in 1 Corinthians 9:24-26 *"Do you not know that in a race all the runners run, but only one gets the prize . . . Everyone who competes goes into strict training . . .I do not run like someone running aimlessly.*" Paul runs with purpose to God's purpose for him.

What does that look like for you and Eileen and Brenda? How do we become spiritually mature and find our purpose? Here is what you do.

This is paraphrasing an email received from a BSF (Bible Study Fellowship) friend: With God helping you, take your everyday, ordinary life—sleeping, eating, going to work and walking around life—and place it before God as an offering. Embrace what God does for you and don't become so well-adjusted to your culture that you fit into it without even thinking or thanking God.

Instead, fix your attention on God. You'll be changed from the inside out. Readily recognize that still small voice and what He wants from you. Quickly respond to it. Don't put it off. Unlike the culture around you, always dragging you down to its level of immaturity, God brings the best out of you and slowly but surely, develops a well-formed maturity in you.

Another friend shared this with us:

Note to Self: "What is my purpose in life?" I asked God.
"What if I told you that you fulfilled it when you took an extra hour to talk to that kid about his life?" said the Voice. "Or when you saved that dog in traffic? Or when you tied your father's shoes for him? Your problem is that you equate purpose with super goal-based achievement."

God isn't interested in your achievements, just your heart for Him.

When you choose to act out of kindness, compassion, and love, you are already aligned with your true purpose in a relationship with Him. No need to look any further. We cannot solve everyone's problem, but we can make a difference for one person. If each of us did that, we would change the world.

The Bible is a love story. God gave us 66 books of the Bible so we would no longer be *"infants, tossed back and forth by the waves, and blown here and there by every wind of teaching and by the cunning and craftiness of men in their deceitful scheming."* (Ephesians 4:14) As mature Christians, when we find that relationship with God we discover that the relationship with God is what He intended as our purpose. Ignorance, prejudice, and injustice will fall away. Matthew Arnold, a 19th century poet and historian said, "if ever the world sees a time when women shall come together purely and simply for the benefit and good of mankind, it will be a power such as the world has never seen."

It is hard to believe that Matthew Arnold understood that concept in the 19th century. Only in the 21st century are we seeing this shift of thought. Shedding our fears, we are discovering power. We are saying, Me too!

From Brenda: Part of that shift occurred for me in Houston, Texas in 1990. It was a warm, Spring Day as women filtered into a meeting. Laughter and easy conversations caught my ear. Hispanic, Women of Color, Asian and Anglo all had an air of expectancy.

It was the second meeting of the Leadership Texas Class of 1990. Approximately 90 women had been selected to participate in this leadership class. They had distinguished themselves in both communities and profession to make a significant contribution throughout Texas. Their titles ranged from Director of Hospital, Investment Manager, Dean of Students, County Judge, Partner in CPA firm, President of College, Attorney and Volunteer Extraordinaire. Taking time from their busy lives, they had arrived in Houston to attend this Leadership seminar and to "reconnect". I felt humbled to be selected as part of the group of 90 in Leadership Texas.

Before us stood Elizabeth Watson, the first female appointed as police chief for a major metropolitan city (Houston) in the U.S. Neither a strident feminist nor shrinking violet, she spoke of changes in the Houston police department: such as her first days of being handed trousers for a uniform as police chief to her recent leave of absence for the birth of her child. As Elizabeth told her story, I realized that there were many stories in the room.

Looking around the room, I began to wonder. Who were the role models who helped these women achieve a "first?" What did older and younger women need to know for leadership development as well as for mentoring in the workplace, community, church or home?

These impressive women freely shared their memories and insights of their mothers and grandmothers who had influenced their lives. At that moment, I decided I could write my dissertation for my Ph.D. program on Critical Incidents in Leadership Development in Women.

As I interviewed the women for my dissertation, across the ethnic lines, the women felt they were not extraordinary. Yet, they had achieved some impressive titles. They felt empowered not by history or the existing culture, but by their heritage of mothers or role models who took active steps toward their deepest desires. Sometimes their mother was not the woman they wanted to model themselves after. Sometimes their environments were oppressive. They generously shared insights on finding an "encircling yes." The mutual strength and encouragements were heady. My dissertation birthed many of the ideas contained in this book. Then life experiences of both Eileen and me confirmed it.

If you are indeed to find your Purpose, you must not try to do it alone. Networking and mentoring with other professionals are a tremendous help. Your "community" of friends is particularly important.

Your personal journey may suffer setbacks. The birds of worry and care will fly above your head. But they don't have to nest there. You have choices and you have control over your decisions. That strength and encouragement on life's timeline can help you remember not only Who you are but Whose you are.

That knowledge leads to your Purpose. Your purpose is a relationship with God. He created us with love and longs for that relationship with us.

From Eileen: You may be wondering why Brenda and I entitled this book, "Fear, Cracked Open"

That is because God sees you as uniquely, fearfully and wonderfully made. He knows you have found an identity or many identities that pull on you in many different life stages. He has helped you through the wilderness. He gave you friends who can help you along in finding fulfillment and purpose. *It has been said that a friend is someone who knows the song in your heart and can sing it back to you even when you have forgotten the words.*

Your friend(s) sees you for what you truly are. Your friend(s) knows that **you're a good egg, even when she knows that you are slightly cracked**.

God can help you to look twice and find clarity over confusion in your purpose, faith over fear and progress over imperfection.

Let's Discuss:

1. God has not given us the spirit of fear, but of power, and of love, and of a sound mind. Are you caught in fear, or are you ready to reach out to the power and love that can help you settle into your Purpose?

2. "That the birds of worry and care fly above your head, that you cannot change. But that you allow them to nest in your hair, that you can change." What worries are you allowing to nest so you are missing out?

3. Do you have friends that believe you're a good egg, even though she/they know you are slightly cracked? Have you shown them gratitude for being there and helping you to sing the song in your heart?

4. It is essential for every generation to know, teach and practice the Bible's truth. Perhaps gaining spiritual maturity is leading you to your Purpose? Is there someone else you should mentor or encourage?

Chapter Twenty-Seven: Connecting with Purpose: The Now and Not Yet

Remember how we were humming Amy Grant's lyrics because they ran true. "No longer what we were before, but not all that we will be." Brenda read a sign in Amsterdam that said, "When it's hot, please dress for the body you have, not the body you want. Thanks"

Recognizing potential, almost fifty years later, Eileen and Brenda are not what they were, but still not all they will be. It is true that we cannot be realistically "anything" we want to be. Hankering to be a surgeon may not match your intellect. But the point is that we can be a lot more of who we already are.

Oprah Winfrey has said this is the very point that life has taught her. So, she now tells "her girls" in the school she supports in Africa that life is recognizing and admitting "who you are," and what makes you happiest rather than allowing the world to make that decision for you.

She found that she enjoyed being out and talking to people, rather than having long lines of book signing where she hardly made eye contact with those purchasing her book. She turned down the areas that brought no joy and amped up the part that she really enjoyed. She said that she knows financially in your 20's you may have to "do" the work that gets you to the point where you financially have some choices. But following your purpose is recognizing who you are rather than what you are supposed to be by the world's standards in whatever life stage you are in.

In a seminar, Brenda told the group that it has been rumored that women speak 20,000 words a day and men speak about 7,000. One woman spoke up quickly and said, "Yes, because we have to repeat everything." The man next to her said, "What?"

As a woman's prerogative, Eilleen and Brenda are repeating a summary. The point of this book is helping you to leave your fear behind and find your purpose. Part of the "Now "is working on getting to the "Not Yet":

*Finding your **Identity** is the act of listening so that you may hear. We have many roles and identities in our life stages: gender expectations, singlehood or parenting, titles or occupations, etc. These often are the world's expectations, and our identities will change as we mature. Life stages will change due to age, health, partnering, etc. To move forward and go toward our purpose means that we first gain alignment with God's intention for us.

*Recognizing that the **Wilderness** will follow success. The wilderness requires 3 things: to humble yourself, to experience it as a proving ground, and to help the Lord see the intent of your heart. Temptations, human limitations, and suffering teach lessons about life. There is purpose in the pain. Through trials and tribulations or in the wilderness experience, we may complain bitterly, indulge in self-pity or rebuke God. Sound familiar? Jesus, instead, obeyed, praised, and drew nearer to the Father.

We are following his model in our life development. Some key points:

 *Let that grape jelly flow with our personal boundaries. You make the decision to let it roll off or to allow it inside your hula hoop as something of consequence. This means bullies don't stand a chance to mess us up in the inevitable **Wilderness** of human time and history. We don't have to let them steal our joy and get inside our head or our boundaries of a hula hoop, whatever the life stage.

* Let humor hone a grateful heart and recognize there is a wonderful **community** in letting a friend help you "see." Your friends think you're a good egg, just slightly cracked. They help you sing your song, even when you forget the words. A community with selected disciples and friends is what Jesus chose when he emerged from the Wilderness. We, too, can benefit health wise and heart wise from "Propellers/encouragers" in our **community** of friends. Choose them well.

* Opt for the still quiet voice rather than burning bushes to find our passion and **Purpose** that God has in mind. We discover who we are and whose we are. This leads us to step out, looking for the Woo-hoo! And the Points of Light that await us.

Jesus said, *"The lamp of the body is the eye. If your eye is healthy, your whole body will be filled with light."* (Matthew 6:22). We want clarity of vision with a healthy viewpoint. We

243

want focus for our vision to step out of the blur and into the light.

Learning to really "see" is a wonderful gift. On a recent birthday (deftly leaving out which one), Brenda decided to go on an Alaskan mission trip. She signed up for a month in July with Alaska Missions to help facilitate college students and put feet to her faith with the Salmon Frenzy on the Kenai, Alaska beaches. On her arrival, these college student leaders (and Brenda) were tasked with climbing Flat Top Mountain outside Anchorage in a team building exercise.

The climb was steep, not necessarily treacherous, but it was demanding and long. It really appeared to get longer to Brenda. The group kept a rapid pace without stopping. She believed the students grew longer legs as the 3-hour trip progressed. She was part of the group that brought up the rear. Occasionally, she did stop to claim that she was looking at the view, but it was really to catch her breath. The mountain was swathed in clouds that had the cat feet of fog, pulling and softly padding strips of clouds hiding the view. Then suddenly the fog would disperse into patches of sunlight.

The clear sunlight revealed velvet green sliding slopes of descending grandeur, length, and beauty. One of the students said, with awe in her voice, "This is just like God. He doesn't let us see the whole journey, . . but occasionally we get these patches of intense beauty. We can't see the whole landscape of our life for the fog, but these brief glimpses of beauty make it worthwhile." This is the idea of 1 Corinthians 13:12 which reminds us that we see through a glass darkly. These divine glimpses on our life journey are what keep us moving up the mountain. We see the Now and hope for the Not Yet.

So many of our fears stem from our self-image and thoughts of beauty. Learning to "see" what is important is what gives us clarity.

From Eileen: I don't think fears concerning self-image end in childhood. I am not a vain person. I do try to look presentable but I'm not phobic about it. A clean blouse, combed hair and usually lipstick and I'm good to go. But recently we were planning a trip to Denver for a visit with our son's family to welcome our new granddaughter Jo Jo and her sister Millie. People warned me about becoming dehydrated in the higher altitude of the Mile High City. Drink lots of water, they said, and be sure to wear a good moisturizer or you will turn into a prune. The thought of becoming one of the California raisins sent me out to buy something for my skin.

Have you shopped for cosmetics recently? Bring your wallet. The promises they made were impressive. Turn back the clock. Be a kid again. Have skin like a baby's butt. Well, maybe not that. But don't become a prune. I paid a whole lot more than I ever planned to. This was an important occasion. I saved a tube for the trip and packed my suitcase.

Once we were checked into our hotel, we had time for hugs and kisses for the whole clan. We settled into bed early, ready for a full day to follow. I made sure to slather on lots of magic cream. At the last moment I decided to apply it only to my neck and upper chest. My face would have to wait for the morning to moisturize—you can't turn back the clock all at once.

I slept poorly that night with lots of twisting and turning with periods of wakefulness and a strange discomfort. When I got out of bed in the morning, my neck was VERY itchy. Looking in the mirror to my horror, I saw masses of hives wherever the cream had been applied. I did not look younger—just multicolored.

Taking an antihistamine was out of the question. I would sleep through the entire visit. But the itch was something I could not ignore. It was spreading. Instead of room service, we scurried to search for a drug store. Benadryl to the rescue.

Three tubes later it was time to head home. I passed the magic cream to my daughter with a warning about allergic reactions. Clearly this beauty regimen was not for me. Looking back, I can see now that I made a mistake. I am comfortable in my own skin. I earned this gray hair. I paid in full for these wrinkles. Why did I want to turn back the clock? I guess vanity comes in all shapes and sizes. From now on, soap and water will do it for me. But I'm keeping a tube of Benadryl around just in case.

(This is Brenda and there must be a disclaimer here. I'm from Dallas. I wear make up to breakfast. I'm a poster child for mascara and eyelashes. If I had to choose one cosmetic to take to a desert island, I would choose mascara. It helps me see better if my eyelashes are curled. My granddaughter Olivia by her insistence must wear bows in her hair and she is two years old. My daughter-in-law, Raven, wisely allows choices that have been carefully honed. But I get the point that Eileen is making. We need to be comfortable in our own skin and learn to "see" what is important.)

We all want to see clearly with 20/20 vision. We want to step out of the blur and have clear vision about what is important to us, what gives us energy, what fulfills us and what God would have us do. Let's face it. We are going to walk through the wilderness in each life stage. We cannot let our deficiencies or past mistakes define us.

With our community of friends, we will conquer to find clarity over confusion. And, in gaining that vital, spiritually mature relationship with God, we will find our purpose that He had in mind, all along. That's how we find purpose. Are you running your life on Sunday School lessons you learned as a child? As a child, we heard stories from the Bible that were valid and made sense to a child. Consequently, are you trying to face the adult trials of the wilderness fueled by the memories you gained as an eight-year-old? It's not Marvel comics with heroes that pop up at opportune times.

Are you facing the loss of a job, marriage partner, or your health with the memory only of the Bible you read and understood as a child? You entered a relationship with God as a child, but you have not stayed a child. As the demands of life have grown in each life stage, so must your relationship with God.

It is time to crack open your fears. Ephesians 4:14 says we need to gain a maturing journey with God, *"Then we will no longer be infants, tossed back and forth by the waves and blown here and there by every wind of teaching and by the cunning and craftiness of men in their deceitful scheming."*

Have you felt tossed back and forth by the wind of every "new" thought and other people's expectations of throwing it out to the universe and "manifesting"? Perhaps that is the cause of some of your fears?

Perhaps that is what has been holding you back. Light exposes darkness. *"For you were once darkness, but now you are light in the Lord."* (Ephesians 5:8) It is time to gain a **mature** faith rather than an elementary one by disciplining ourselves to go to the correct source for answers to our questions. Allow the Lord to talk to you via the Bible and to sharpen your strength. Consistently exercise discipline to find your faith.

The Lord is waiting on you at the well, just like He was for the Samaritan woman. He has eternal living water for you, too. There she was, just strolling down the street. It was high noon. It was a deserted time of the day so she could avoid the judgment of the other women. She wasn't just a woman; she was *that kind* of woman with a few (at least six) mistakes in her past. Clearly Jesus was expecting her, and he asked her for a drink. She doesn't believe it! "You are a Jew, and I am a Samaritan woman. How can you ask me for a drink (Jews don't associate with Samaritans) John 4:9. Jesus replies with the offer of living water. He also lets her know that he knows she has had five husbands and is living with a sixth man. Oops! She changes the subject and starts a debate on theology. She wasn't afraid to ask him questions. She is thirsty for the truth.

When her eyes were opened and she saw Christ for who He really was, she became a believer. She rushed back to the town, *"Come see a man who told me everything I ever did. Could this be the Christ?"* John 4: 28-29. We think it is extraordinary that the men of her city listened to her, a shady woman. But they ran to find Jesus.

They saw something in her that couldn't be contained--Christ in her. The Samaritans came to Jesus and begged him to stay. He stayed two days in Samaria. And because of his words, many became believers (John 4:40-41).

Are you able to identify with the Samaritan woman and have many questions burning in your heart? Are you ready to mature in your faith? Are you ready to leave the wilderness of fear to find out what your purpose really is? Does your soul thirst for a relationship with the living God? Psalm 42:2 says,

"My soul thirsts for God, for the living God. When can I go and meet with God?"

The answer is in James 1:5, "If *any of you lacks wisdom, he should ask God, who gives generously to all without finding fault, and it will be given to him."*

No fault. For free. Finding your purpose? Ask and it will be given when you get aligned with Whose you are. Look twice. He's waiting. Redesign or decline.

If he could wait for a bad girl of the Bible, he can wait for you. Does the fear of the lack of control hold you back? Almost every story in the Bible dealt with stress, famine, war or pestilence. David had a King chasing to kill him in his early life and a son who mobilized an army to come after him in his later life. The mother of Moses had a baby that she floated on a basket in the Nile with crocodiles rather than have the Pharaoh murder her baby boy. On the way to Rome and potential execution, Paul was shipwrecked. How aggravating. We can identify with that. It was bad and only seemed to get worse. The world then and now seems to spin out of control. It was the Now and the Not Yet. Are we to be bitter or better?

Each person learned not to be distracted by things out of control, but to place their deepest, most entrenched, fear at the feet of God. The only thing that has remained certain since the beginning of time is God. When we go through a life of panic, chaos and lack of control, we are frustrated because we have not tapped into the peace that passes understanding that God offers.

Our past does not determine our future. Step out of the blur. Take His hand.

Gain focus and clarity, not vision blurred by irrational fears.

We gain the peace of God, not the peace of circumstances being erased. Do Eileen and Brenda believe this? Yes, because we have seen God in action. Uncertainty has always been and always will be with us.

Recently on a trip to India, Brenda saw these words by Ghandi on the wall of his former apartment. "Man becomes what he believes himself to be. If I keep saying I cannot do a certain thing, I may end up by really becoming incapable of doing it. To the contrary, if I believe I can do it, I shall surely acquire the capability to do it, even if I can't at the beginning."

And Ghandi persevered to help India win the impossible goal of its freedom despite imprisonment and personal struggle.

Fears pop up and isolate.

 But the people of faith can have a level of serenity that passes understanding. Your story, no matter your age or life stage is just a beginning.

Can we really trust when the turbulence of the wilderness is great? Cowgirl up! We are ready for the challenge because we are certain that God is with us.

We can give ourselves permission to spend time only with those we enjoy. We can find splendor in the grass or the sunset. We can integrate into ourselves a deeper sense of who we are and whose we are. We can train ourselves to be grateful for the Now while hoping for the Not Yet. We can Redesign, not decline.

What do you think?

We hope this book has helped you to look twice and have your **Fear Cracked Open**. Panic is replaced by prayer; paralysis replaced by productivity. Purpose rather than pain. You are discovering the You that you deserve.

We hope you have enjoyed some of the humor along the way so you can recognize your (and our) progress, not imperfection.

We pray that you will use this book individually and as a group study to give you confidence and joy to move toward your deepest desires, passion and purpose that both delights you and inspires others.

Redesign or decline! Do not drive a car that only moves in reverse. Forward, ho!

Finally, our hope is that you, too, find a true friend who thinks you're a good egg, even though she knows you're slightly cracked! Woo-hoo!

Hugs
Brenda and Eileen

Made in the USA
Coppell, TX
13 November 2023

24175574R00144